GROWING GRACEFULLY

DR. KIRAN GAMBALA

INDIA • SINGAPORE • MALAYSIA

CONTENTS

Chapter 1

INTRODUCTION

1.1 WELCOME TO THE JOURNEY

"Little Girls With Dreams Become Women With Vision."

In the quiet hush of dawn, amidst whispered prayers and tender embraces, she arrived—a radiant star born into our waiting arms. Her first cry, a melody that echoed with promise and hope, filled the room with a symphony of joy. In that miraculous moment, as I held her delicate form against my chest, waves of overwhelming love washed over me, mingled with tears of gratitude that flowed freely.

She, our daughter, a testament to the miracle of life and the embodiment of all our dreams. Her arrival marked not just a birth, but a celebration of strength, resilience, and the enduring power of love. Every heartbeat resonated with the rhythm of new beginnings, and each breath drawn in awe of the beauty cradled in my arms.

As sunlight streamed through the window, illuminating her tiny features and casting a gentle glow upon her peaceful slumber, I knew that her presence would forever bless our lives. With her birth, we welcomed not only a daughter but a beacon of hope, a promise of tomorrow's possibilities.

In her eyes, I see the future—a canvas yet to be painted, filled with adventures, laughter, and dreams waiting to unfold. Her existence is a gift beyond measure, and with each passing moment, I am filled with the profound privilege of witnessing her grow, thrive, and become the woman she is destined to be.

BUT

In certain uncivilised societies, girls are often perceived as a burden due to deep-seated cultural, social, and economic factors. Here are some common reasons why this perception exists:

Economic Factors: In agrarian or resource-scarce communities, girls may be seen as less economically productive compared to boys. They are sometimes viewed as liabilities because of the dowry system prevalent in some cultures, where substantial sums of money, goods, or property are demanded by the groom's family.

Patriarchal Norms: Many societies uphold patriarchal values where males are considered more valuable for continuing the family lineage, inheriting property, and providing financial support. This can lead to devaluing girls from birth, seen as destined to marry out of their family and potentially draining their family's resources through dowry payments.

Educational and Career Opportunities: In some cultures, girls are given less access to education and fewer opportunities for career advancement, reinforcing the idea that they are less capable or important than boys.

Gender-Based Violence: Girls may be at a higher risk of violence, including neglect, infanticide, or abandonment, particularly in areas where son preference is strong. This can be exacerbated by factors such as economic pressures or traditional beliefs about the roles and capabilities of girls.

Cultural and Religious Beliefs: Traditional beliefs and religious practices may perpetuate the idea that girls are inferior or less valuable than boys, impacting their social status, opportunities, and overall treatment within the community.

These factors contribute to a societal mindset where girls are seen as burdens rather than valued members deserving of equal rights and opportunities.

YES

There still exists differentiation between girl and boy children in various societies around the world. These differences manifest in multiple areas including education, health, social expectations, and economic opportunities. These disparities are evident in many key areas.

Education

Access to education remains a significant challenge for many girls around the world. Cultural norms, economic constraints, and safety concerns often result in girls being less likely to attend school compared to boys. Even when girls do attend school, the quality of education they receive can be inferior due to a lack of resources and adequate facilities. This educational disparity hampers their ability to acquire the skills and knowledge needed for future opportunities, perpetuating a cycle of inequality.

Health

Healthcare access is another area where girls face significant disadvantages. In many societies, girls have less access to healthcare services, leading to higher rates of malnutrition, disease, and mortality. Reproductive health is particularly neglected, with girls facing substantial barriers to accessing necessary services and education. This increases the risks of early pregnancy and sexually transmitted infections, which can have long-term impacts on their health and well-being.

Social Expectations

Societal expectations often dictate that girls should conform to traditional gender roles, limiting their personal and professional growth. These roles can restrict girls' opportunities to explore interests and careers that fall outside of conventional norms. Furthermore, in many cultures, girls are more likely to be married off at a young age, which significantly impacts their education and health, trapping them in cycles of dependency and limited opportunities.

Economic Opportunities

The disparity in economic opportunities between girls and boys is stark. Women face greater challenges in entering the workforce and achieving equal pay compared to men. Cultural and societal norms often discourage girls from pursuing careers, especially in fields traditionally dominated by men. Additionally, legal and societal barriers frequently prevent women from attaining economic independence, restricting their ability to make financial decisions and participate fully in economic activities.

Social and Cultural Norms

Gender-based violence and discrimination remain pervasive issues affecting girls and women. Girls are often more vulnerable to various forms of violence, including domestic violence, sexual harassment, and trafficking. These experiences not only cause immediate harm but also have long-lasting effects on their mental and physical health. Moreover, girls and women are significantly underrepresented in leadership positions across politics, business, and academia, which further reinforces their marginalisation and limits their influence on decision-making processes.

MY HEART IS THROBBING WITH PAIN, MY EYES WITH TEARS, AND MY MIND WITH QUESTIONS

AM I NOT GOD'S CREATION?
AM I NOT CREATED WITH LOVE TO DISTRIBUTE LOVE?

AM I A BURDEN TO THE UNIVERSE THAT CREATED ME?

AM I SO UNWANTED?

AM I SO WORTHLESS?

AM I AN ORPHAN WITH KIN AND KEEN?

IS THERE NO ONE TO LOVE ME AND WELCOME ME?

I am wondering how many battles I should fight,

For the right to learn and the chance to be bright.

Against the norms that hold me down,

And expectations that make me drown.

I am wondering how many battles I should fight,

For healthcare that meets my needs,

For the same care and love, to plant my seeds.

In the face of violence, I stand tall.

Demanding safety and respect for all.

I am wondering how many battles I should fight,

To shatter the glass ceilings high,

For equal pay and the right to fly.

Against the roles that box me in,

For the freedom to dream, to lose, to win.

I am wondering how many battles I should fight,

To create a world where no hearts break.

A world where I can live with pride,

No longer forced to hide or abide.

I am wondering how many battles I should fight,

For a future bright and fair,

Where every girl can breathe freely.

How many battles must I face?

Until we live in an equal place.

I AM WONDERING HOW MANY BATTLES I SHOULD WIN

While progress has been made in many areas, achieving true gender equality remains a work in progress. Addressing the disparities between girls and boys requires ongoing, concerted efforts from all sectors of society. Ensuring that every child, regardless of gender, has equal opportunities to succeed is essential for building a just and equitable world. Continued advocacy, policy changes, and community support are necessary to dismantle the barriers that perpetuate gender inequality and create a brighter future for all.

1.2 WHAT TO EXPECT

While various supports are essential for a girl child's growth, I am particularly emphasising the importance of nurturing emotional intelligence and resilience. These two components are foundational for her overall well-being, helping her navigate life's challenges with confidence and grace. By focusing on emotional intelligence, we equip her with the ability to understand and manage her emotions, fostering empathy and strong social skills. Building resilience, on the other hand, ensures she can recover from setbacks and adapt to change, maintaining a positive outlook despite difficulties. This dual emphasis not only supports her current development but also lays the groundwork for a fulfilling and empowered future.

This book on supporting a girl child's emotional intelligence will provide a comprehensive overview of emotional intelligence (EI) and its significance in her development. It will delve into the core components of EI—self-awareness, self-regulation, motivation, empathy, and social skills—and explain why these are essential for her overall well-being and success. Readers can expect detailed insights into the emotional and psychological developmental stages of a girl child, offering age-specific guidance to help parents and caregivers understand and meet her needs effectively.

The book will feature practical strategies and activities designed to foster emotional intelligence, including techniques for recognising and naming emotions, developing empathy, managing stress, and resolving conflicts. These activities, such as role-playing, journaling, and mindfulness exercises, will make learning engaging and effective.

Parenting techniques will be a significant focus, with guidance on nurturing a daughter's emotional growth through effective communication, active listening, and modelling emotional intelligence in daily interactions.

The book will provide tools for creating an emotionally supportive environment that encourages open dialogue and expression. It will address common emotional challenges faced by girls, such as dealing with peer pressure, building self-esteem, and navigating societal expectations, offering practical tools and tips for managing these challenges constructively. Real-life case studies and examples will illustrate key concepts, making the material relatable and understandable.

Additionally, the book will include a collection of resources and tools, such as worksheets, checklists, and activities, to help parents and caregivers implement the strategies in everyday life. Focused guidance on building resilience and confidence will emphasise the importance of a growth mindset, learning from failures, and maintaining a positive outlook. The book will also advise on fostering healthy relationships with peers, family, and mentors, teaching girls how to build and maintain positive connections, set boundaries, and navigate social dynamics effectively.

Lastly, promoting a balanced lifestyle that includes attention to both mental and physical health will be addressed, with tips on encouraging physical activity, healthy eating, sufficient sleep, and accessing mental health resources. By covering these key areas, the book aims to equip parents and caregivers with the knowledge and tools needed to support their daughters' emotional intelligence, ensuring they grow up to be strong, resilient, and content individuals.

Chapter 2

UNDERSTANDING EMOTIONAL INTELLIGENCE

2.1 CELEBRATING THE MASCULINE ENERGY

Absolutely, hats off indeed! The men who positively impact a woman's life play crucial roles as fathers, brothers, partners, friends, mentors, and beyond. Their support, encouragement, understanding, and respect contribute immensely to women's growth, achievements, and well-being. Whether through love, guidance, empowerment, or simply being there, these men help create environments where women can thrive, pursue their dreams, and find fulfilment. Recognising and appreciating their contributions celebrates the strength of meaningful connections and the importance of mutual support in building a more inclusive and compassionate world.

"Kudos to the men who break barriers to empower pearls."

In your embrace, a daughter finds her wings,

Your love, a beacon through life's uncertain things.

With every step, your belief unwavering and true,

You empower her dreams to take flight and pursue.

"Kudos to the men who break barriers to empower pearls."

A brother's strength, a shield from doubt's abyss,

In your laughter, her spirit finds its bliss.

Hand in hand, you conquer worlds with glee.

A bond unbroken, bound by destiny's decree.

"Kudos to the men who break barriers to empower pearls."

In your eyes, she sees love's gentle embrace.

A partner's touch, a sanctuary, a safe place.

Together, you dance through life's intricate design,

In your union, her heart finds solace, divine.

"Kudos to the men who break barriers to empower pearls."

Friends like stars, guiding her path with light,

Through laughter and tears, your bond shines bright.

With every word, a melody of courage and cheer,

You paint life's canvas with hues of friendship, dear.

"Kudos to the men who break barriers to empower pearls."

A mentor's wisdom, a compass in the storm,

Guiding her steps through wisdom's form.

In your teachings, her mind finds wisdom's key,

A beacon of knowledge, unlocking futures, free.

"Kudos to the men who break barriers to empower pearls."

To the men who defy limits, break down walls,

Who champions her spirit, heeds passion's calls.

Across boundaries, their support unfurls.

For they uplift her world, with courage that swirls.

"A Girl's First Love Is Always Her Father."

In a world that thrives on balance, celebrating the unique contributions of men who uplift, nurture, and champion the women in their lives is a powerful acknowledgement of the symbiotic connection that supports collective progress. Masculine energy, when channelled with empathy, respect, and understanding, creates an atmosphere in which women feel empowered, valued, and inspired to reach new heights. Men who assume roles as fathers, brothers, partners, friends, and mentors bring a blend of strength and sensitivity that is both protective and liberating. This duality enables women to move forward with courage, knowing they have advocates who will not only stand by them but will also celebrate their successes and nurture their aspirations.

Historically, society has witnessed numerous examples of men who actively participated in breaking down barriers for women, standing alongside them in their journey toward equality. Today, this support is more crucial than ever. With the roles and identities of women constantly evolving, the positive masculine presence offers a foundation of reassurance and encouragement. Men who celebrate women's achievements, recognise their capabilities, and respect their autonomy foster an environment that reinforces women's sense of self-worth and fortifies their belief in their potential. This collaboration builds trust, affirming that support can come from all fronts and that one's ambitions do not need to be limited by gender-based constraints.

One of the most impactful aspects of this supportive masculine energy is its capacity to challenge outdated gender norms and stereotypes. In stepping into these roles, men show that strength and empathy are not mutually exclusive. When men openly express their pride in the women they care for, they break down stereotypes that have traditionally relegated women to certain roles and expectations. They demonstrate that masculinity can be both powerful and gentle, capable of standing up for a loved one while also stepping back to let her take centre stage. Such actions convey a powerful message to younger generations, teaching boys and girls alike that respect, kindness, and equality form the bedrock of all healthy relationships.

Furthermore, this celebration of masculine support highlights the transformative power of mentorship. For a young girl, having a father, brother, or mentor who believes in her abilities can be life-changing. This belief fosters self-assurance, encouraging her to step out of her comfort zone and take on challenges with determination. Similarly, a woman navigating her career, education, or personal growth journey will find a world of difference in having a male mentor who not only advises her but also actively removes obstacles, helps her network, and advocates for her ideas and contributions. This backing transforms possibilities into realities, expanding her opportunities and horizons. The courage a woman gathers from such supportive men is not just about achieving her goals but also about learning to trust in herself and her instincts.

The impact of these relationships extends beyond personal growth and empowerment; it also contributes to a more inclusive and compassionate world. In today's interconnected society, collaboration between men and women is essential for addressing the complex challenges we face. By standing together in mutual respect, both genders can create solutions that are more innovative, inclusive, and reflective of the diverse perspectives they bring to the table. This synergy fosters a culture of appreciation and gratitude, where differences are not only accepted but celebrated. As men and women support each other's journeys, they build a foundation for a society that values compassion over competition and collaboration over division.

Celebrating masculine energy in this way reminds us of the positive ripple effect that men can have when they stand with women. Each act of support and understanding strengthens the bonds within families, workplaces, and communities. These acts may range from grand gestures to everyday moments, but each one reinforces the idea that progress is most meaningful when achieved together. In a world often divided, these connections are the bridges that remind us of our shared humanity.

In conclusion, recognising and appreciating the masculine energy that elevates women is not just about gratitude—it is a call to continue nurturing these relationships. It is about encouraging more men to embrace roles that foster equality, support, and shared success. This celebration acknowledges that our world grows stronger when men and women work together, not in isolation. By valuing these contributions, we create a culture that not only honours the achievements of individuals but also cherishes the connections that make such achievements possible. As we celebrate masculine energy, we honour the vital role men play in creating an inclusive, compassionate world where everyone has the opportunity to thrive. In this collective journey toward mutual empowerment, every supportive relationship adds a chapter to a story of resilience, unity, and shared progress.

2.2 WHAT IS EMOTIONAL INTELLIGENCE?

Emotional intelligence (EI) is the ability to understand, manage, and effectively express one's own emotions, as well as to navigate and influence the emotions of others. It encompasses self-awareness, self-regulation, motivation, empathy, and social skills, all of which contribute to personal and professional success. EI enables individuals to build stronger relationships, communicate more effectively, resolve conflicts, and lead with empathy and understanding. Developing EI involves practices such as self-reflection, mindfulness, active listening, and seeking feedback. By enhancing emotional intelligence, individuals can improve their decision-making, foster healthier interactions, and achieve greater overall well-being.

2.3 THE CORE COMPONENTS OF EMOTIONAL INTELLIGENCE

Self-Awareness and Emotional Intelligence

Self-awareness is a cornerstone of emotional intelligence (EI), which involves the ability to recognise, understand, manage, and influence both our own emotions and the emotions of others. The relationship between self-awareness and EI is profound and multifaceted, influencing various aspects of personal and professional life.

Defining Self-Awareness

Self-awareness is the ability to accurately perceive one's own emotions in the moment and understand one's tendencies across situations. It encompasses recognising how our emotions affect our thoughts and behaviours, understanding our strengths and weaknesses, and possessing a grounded sense of our values and motives.

Foundation of Emotional Understanding

At the heart of EI is the capacity to understand and interpret emotions—both our own and those of others. Self-awareness lays the groundwork for this by enabling us to identify and comprehend our emotional states. This understanding is critical because it allows us to predict how our emotions influence our behaviour and decisions. For instance, recognising when we feel stressed can help us take steps to calm ourselves before responding to a challenging situation, leading to more measured and effective responses.

Informed Self-Regulation

Self-regulation, another key component of EI, involves managing our emotions in healthy ways. Self-awareness is essential here because it helps us recognise our emotional triggers and responses. By understanding these triggers, we can develop strategies to regulate our emotions, such as deep breathing, positive self-talk, or taking a break when needed. This ability to control our impulses and stay composed under pressure is vital for maintaining personal and professional relationships and achieving long-term goals.

Enhanced Motivation

Understanding what drives and motivates us is another aspect of EI that is deeply connected to self-awareness. By being aware of our inner desires, aspirations, and emotional triggers, we can align our goals with our intrinsic motivations. This alignment fosters greater enthusiasm, persistence, and resilience. For example, a self-aware individual might recognise that they are motivated by a sense of achievement and thus set challenging yet attainable goals that inspire and drive them.

Empathy Development

Empathy, the ability to understand and share the feelings of others, is greatly enhanced by self-awareness. When we are attuned to our own emotions, we can better appreciate and relate to the emotional experiences of others. This empathy enables us to build stronger, more supportive relationships and to navigate social complexities with sensitivity and understanding. By recognising our own emotional states, we become more adept at interpreting the emotions of those around us, fostering deeper connections and more effective communication.

Improved Social Skills

Effective social interactions and relationships are another crucial aspect of EI. Self-awareness plays a significant role in developing social skills because it helps us understand how we come across to others and how our emotions influence our interactions. This awareness allows us to adjust our behaviour to suit different social contexts and to communicate more clearly and empathetically. For instance, a self-aware leader can recognise when their stress might be affecting their team and take steps to address it, thereby maintaining a positive and productive work environment.

2.4 THE FIVE PILLARS OF EMOTIONAL INTELLIGENCE

The Five Pillars of Emotional Intelligence

1. **Self-Awareness**: Self-awareness is the cornerstone of emotional intelligence. It involves the ability to recognise and understand one's own emotions, strengths, weaknesses, values, and motivations. Individuals with high self-awareness are attuned to their feelings, allowing them to gauge how these emotions influence their thoughts, behaviours, and interactions with others. This awareness

is crucial for personal growth, as it enables individuals to identify areas for improvement and understand the underlying reasons behind their reactions. Self-awareness is typically developed through self-reflection, mindfulness, and regular assessment of one's responses in different situations. By honing self-awareness, individuals can make more intentional choices, remain grounded, and align their actions with their values and goals.

2. **Self-Regulation**: Self-regulation, or emotional control, refers to the ability to manage and redirect disruptive emotions and impulses, maintaining composure even in stressful or challenging situations. It involves the practice of pausing before reacting, allowing individuals to think critically rather than acting impulsively. Those who excel in self-regulation can navigate complex emotional landscapes, such as anger, frustration, or disappointment, without letting these feelings affect their judgement. This ability is essential in both personal and professional settings, where impulsive reactions can lead to misunderstandings or conflicts. Self-regulation is nurtured through strategies such as deep breathing, mindfulness, and emotional reframing, which allow individuals to stay calm and focused even when under pressure.

3. **Motivation**: Motivation within the context of emotional intelligence refers to an internal drive that goes beyond external rewards like money or status. Emotionally intelligent individuals are motivated by a sense of purpose, achievement, and the desire to grow personally and professionally. They set challenging yet achievable goals and approach tasks with enthusiasm and persistence. High motivation also encourages individuals to remain resilient in the face of setbacks, viewing obstacles as opportunities for growth rather than deterrents. This intrinsic motivation promotes long-term commitment and perseverance, key qualities

for achieving sustained success. Individuals can build motivation by aligning their goals with personal values, setting incremental milestones, and celebrating small wins along the way.

4. **Empathy**: Empathy, often described as the heart of emotional intelligence, is the ability to understand and share the feelings of others. Empathetic individuals can put themselves in others' shoes, viewing situations from alternative perspectives. This capacity fosters compassion, which is crucial for building trust, resolving conflicts, and creating inclusive environments. Empathy allows individuals to respond to others' needs with understanding and support, creating stronger connections and improving collaboration. Developing empathy involves active listening, remaining non-judgemental, and being genuinely curious about others' experiences. By enhancing their empathy, individuals not only improve their interpersonal relationships but also promote a sense of community and belonging in their surroundings.

5. **Social Skills**: Social skills encompass a range of competencies that enable individuals to interact harmoniously with others, such as effective communication, conflict resolution, and teamwork. Those with strong social skills are adept at interpreting non-verbal cues, adjusting their communication style based on the audience, and handling conflicts in a constructive manner. They also excel at networking and building relationships, which are valuable skills in both personal and professional settings. Social skills are built over time through intentional practice, including active listening, assertive communication, and a focus on building rapport. Strong social skills help individuals navigate social dynamics smoothly, promoting cooperation, collaboration, and mutual respect.

2.5 THE ROLE OF EMOTIONAL INTELLIGENCE IN SUCCESS

Emotional intelligence plays a pivotal role in achieving personal, social, and professional success. In the workplace, for instance, EI can influence job performance, leadership effectiveness, and career advancement. Leaders with high emotional intelligence create positive work environments by inspiring, motivating, and understanding their team members. They handle conflicts with poise, encourage open communication, and foster a culture of mutual respect. For employees, EI contributes to better stress management, adaptability, and the ability to work well within a team. In personal relationships, emotional intelligence strengthens bonds by enabling individuals to communicate openly, empathise with others, and resolve disagreements constructively.

Individuals with high emotional intelligence are better equipped to navigate life's complexities and manage their mental well-being. They have a greater capacity to handle stress, manage change, and bounce back from adversity. Their ability to understand and manage their emotions reduces the likelihood of burnout and enhances their overall life satisfaction. By recognising emotional patterns and adopting coping strategies, they can maintain a balanced perspective and approach life's challenges with resilience and optimism.

2.6 DEVELOPING EMOTIONAL INTELLIGENCE

Enhancing emotional intelligence is a gradual, ongoing process that requires self-reflection, practice, and a commitment to personal growth. Some effective methods for developing EI include:

- **Self-Reflection** Regular self-reflection helps individuals assess their emotional responses, identify triggers, and understand how their emotions influence their behaviour. Reflecting on experiences, both positive and negative, fosters deeper self-awareness and guides future responses.

- **Mindfulness**: Practising mindfulness enables individuals to stay present and focused, helping them observe their emotions without judgement. This practice encourages self-regulation by allowing individuals to pause before reacting, enhancing emotional stability.

- **Active Listening**: Active listening is essential for empathy and social skills. By giving others undivided attention, individuals can better understand their perspectives, validate their emotions, and respond more thoughtfully.

- **Seeking Feedback**: Constructive feedback from others provides insights into how one's emotional responses and behaviours are perceived. Feedback can reveal blind spots, helping individuals identify areas where they can further develop their EI.

- **Emotion Journals**: Keeping an emotion journal allows individuals to document their feelings, reactions, and thoughts about specific events. This practice helps in recognising emotional patterns, leading to greater self-awareness and control.

2.7 THE IMPACT OF EMOTIONAL INTELLIGENCE ON WELL-BEING

Emotional intelligence has a profound impact on an individual's overall well-being. By fostering self-awareness and self-regulation, individuals can reduce stress, improve mental health, and increase life satisfaction. Enhanced empathy and social skills enable stronger, more fulfilling relationships, promoting a sense of belonging and support. Motivation, rooted in personal values and intrinsic goals, brings a sense of purpose and accomplishment. Together, these factors contribute to a more balanced, resilient, and fulfilling life.

In conclusion, emotional intelligence is not only a key determinant of success but also a foundation for a more harmonious and empathetic society. By cultivating self-awareness, self-regulation, motivation, empathy, and social skills, individuals can create positive change within themselves and in their relationships with others. Developing emotional intelligence is a lifelong journey, but its rewards—greater well-being, deeper connections, and personal fulfilment—make the investment worthwhile.

2.8 STAGES OF EMOTIONAL INTELLIGENCE

Emotional intelligence (EI) evolves and grows across a person's lifetime. Here is a general outline of its stages from infancy to old age:

1. Infancy (0-2 years)

- **Emotion Awareness**: Infants start to recognise their own emotions and those of their caregivers. They express basic feelings such as joy, anger, sadness, and fear.

- **Attachment and Bonding**: Secure attachments with caregivers create a sense of safety and love, laying the groundwork for emotional growth.

- **Emotion Regulation**: Infants begin learning self-soothing techniques, often aided by their caregivers.

2. Early Childhood (3-5 Years)

- **Emotion Understanding**: Children start to identify and label their own emotions and those of others, and they develop basic empathy by recognising others' feelings.

- **Social Interaction**: Play and interaction with peers help children learn to share, take turns, and resolve conflicts.
- **Emotion Expression**: Children become more expressive and start to use words to describe their feelings.

3. Middle Childhood (6-12 Years)

- **Complex Emotions**: Children understand more complex emotions such as guilt, shame, and pride, and they begin to grasp the reasons behind these emotions.
- **Empathy and Perspective-Taking**: They develop a better ability to empathise and understand others' perspectives.
- **Emotion Regulation**: They gain improved control over their emotions, employing more sophisticated strategies to manage their feelings.

4. Adolescence (13-18 Years)

- **Identity and Self-Awareness**: Adolescents explore their own identities and become more self-aware, reflecting on their emotions and motivations.
- **Social Awareness**: Increased sensitivity to social dynamics and peer relationships, with a deeper understanding of social norms and expectations.
- **Emotional Independence**: Adolescents begin to rely more on themselves for emotional regulation, though peer support remains significant.

5. Early Adulthood (19-35 Years)

- **Emotional Stability**: Emotional regulation becomes more consistent, with adults managing stress and emotions in a balanced way.

- **Relationship Management**: They build and maintain healthy relationships through effective communication, empathy, and conflict resolution.

- **Empathy and Social Responsibility**: Adults develop greater empathy and consideration for others' well-being, contributing to society and community.

6. Middle Adulthood (36-60 Years)

- **Emotional Wisdom**: A deeper understanding of emotions and their impacts emerges, often leading to increased patience, reflection, and tolerance.

- **Mentorship and Guidance**: Many take on roles as mentors or advisers, using their emotional intelligence to guide younger generations.

- **Balance and Fulfillment**: Focus on achieving personal and professional fulfillment and finding balance in life.

7. Late Adulthood (60+ Years)

- **Reflective and Philosophical**: Older adults often reflect on their lives and the emotions they have experienced, gaining greater wisdom and perspective.

- **Acceptance and Adaptation**: They develop acceptance of life's changes and losses, focusing on adaptation and finding peace.

- **Emotional Legacy**: Emphasis on leaving an emotional legacy, such as imparting wisdom, maintaining relationships, and nurturing family ties.

Throughout these stages, the development of emotional intelligence is shaped by individual experiences, relationships, cultural contexts, and personal growth, each stage building upon the previous to contribute to overall emotional maturity and intelligence.

Chapter 3

DEVELOPMENTAL STAGES OF EMOTIONAL INTELLIGENCE

3.1 EMOTIONAL AND PSYCHOLOGICAL DEVELOPMENT IN INFANCY

Children begin to feel emotions from birth, although the complexity and range of emotions develop over time.

Newborns (0-2 months): Newborns express basic emotions such as distress, contentment, and interest. They can show signs of discomfort (crying) and contentment (calmness, cooing).

Infants (2-6 months): As infants grow, they start to show more distinct emotions such as joy (smiling, laughing), sadness, anger, and surprise. They begin to respond to caregivers' expressions and interactions.

Older Infants (6-12 months): Around this age, infants develop a wider range of emotions, including fear and shyness. They start to experience separation anxiety and show a preference for familiar people.

Toddlers (1-3 years): Toddlers begin to develop more complex emotions such as empathy, embarrassment, pride, and shame. They start to recognise and respond to others' emotions and develop a sense of self.

Preschoolers (3-5 years): During this stage, children's emotional range continues to expand. They learn to better understand and express their feelings, regulate their emotions, and develop social skills such as sharing and cooperation.

While emotions are present from birth, their expression and understanding become more sophisticated as children grow and develop.

Supporting the emotional development of children from birth is essential for their overall well-being and future success. By providing a nurturing and responsive environment, caregivers help children develop the emotional skills necessary for a happy, healthy and fulfilling life.

Newborns, during the first two months of life, primarily experience and express basic emotions. These emotions are essential for their survival and help them communicate their needs to caregivers. Here is a more detailed look at how newborns express these basic emotions:

1. Distress

- **Crying**: Crying is the primary way newborns communicate distress. It can signal various needs such as hunger, a wet diaper, discomfort, or the need for sleep. Different cries can indicate different types of distress, and parents often learn to distinguish between them over time.
- **Fussing**: Fussing is another form of expressing distress. It can involve whimpering, squirming, and appearing unsettled.

2. Contentment

- **Calmness**: Newborns express contentment through a state of calmness. When their needs are met, they may appear relaxed, with their muscles loose and their facial expressions serene.

- **Cooing**: Around 6-8 weeks, some newborns start making cooing sounds, which are soft, pleasant vocalisations. Cooing is often a sign of contentment and can occur during interactions with caregivers or while the baby is exploring their environment.

- **Smiling**: Although true social smiling usually starts around 6-8 weeks, some newborns may show early smiles, often during sleep or in response to comfort.

3. Interest

- **Wide-Eyed Gazing**: Newborns show interest by focusing intently on faces, objects, and movements. They often prefer high-contrast patterns and faces, especially those of their caregivers.

- **Tracking Movements**: As their vision develops, newborns begin to track moving objects with their eyes, showing curiosity and interest.

- **Quiet Alert State**: During periods of quiet alertness, newborns are calm but awake and attentive, often looking around and observing their surroundings.

Caregiver Responses to Newborn Emotions

Caregivers play a vital role in nurturing a child's emotional development by providing responsive and consistent support, which fosters security and trust. They can respond to distress by identifying and addressing the baby's needs, using soothing techniques, and offering consistent comfort. Encouraging contentment involves frequent physical contact, gentle interactions, and ensuring a comfortable environment. Stimulating interest includes visual stimulation, interactive play, and supervised tummy time. Caregivers also provide emotional support through responsive caregiving, physical comfort, and creating secure environments with consistent routines and safe spaces. By modelling and teaching emotional skills, such as labelling emotions and demonstrating healthy coping strategies, caregivers guide children in emotional regulation. Encouraging social interaction and fostering independence and confidence through exploration and decision-making opportunities further support emotional growth. By listening, validating emotions, and teaching conflict resolution, caregivers create an emotionally safe space, helping build a strong foundation for the child's emotional well-being and resilience.

3.2 IMPORTANCE OF PAYING ATTENTION TO THE EMOTIONAL DEVELOPMENT OF CHILDREN

Paying attention to and supporting the emotions of children from birth is essential for their overall development and well-being. Responsive caregiving fosters a secure attachment, building trust and emotional security, which are foundational for healthy emotional and social development. Early emotional support helps children learn to regulate their emotions, express themselves effectively, and develop empathy and social skills necessary for positive relationships. It also promotes cognitive development and resilience, reducing anxiety and stress, leading to better mental health and academic success. By providing consistent, affectionate, and positive interactions, caregivers play a crucial role in nurturing the child's emotional intelligence, setting the stage for their future happiness and success in personal and professional life.

Paying attention to and providing support for the emotions of children from birth is crucial for several reasons:

1. Building a Secure Attachment

- **Emotional Bonding**: Responsive caregiving helps form a secure attachment between the child and caregiver. This bond is foundational for the child's emotional and social development.

- **Trust and Security**: When caregivers consistently meet a child's emotional needs, the child learns to trust others and feel secure in their environment.

2. Healthy Emotional Development

- **Emotional Regulation**: Early support helps children learn to manage and regulate their emotions. This skill is essential for coping with stress and challenges later in life.

- **Emotional Expression**: Encouraging children to express their emotions healthily helps them understand and communicate their feelings effectively.

3. Social Skills and Relationships

- **Empathy and Compassion**: By acknowledging and responding to a child's emotions, caregivers teach empathy and compassion. Children learn to recognise and respond to the emotions of others.

- **Interpersonal Skills**: Early emotional support helps children develop the social skills needed for forming positive relationships with peers and adults.

4. Cognitive Development

- **Learning and Exploration**: Emotional security promotes exploration and learning. Children who feel safe are more likely to engage with their environment, fostering cognitive development.

- **Problem-Solving Skills**: Understanding and managing emotions contributes to better problem-solving and decision-making abilities.

5. Mental Health and Well-Being

- **Reduced Anxiety and Stress**: Supportive emotional care reduces anxiety and stress in children, contributing to better mental health outcomes.

- **Resilience**: Children who receive emotional support are more resilient and better able to cope with adversities and setbacks.

6. Behavioural Outcomes

- **Positive Behaviour**: Children who feel understood and supported are less likely to exhibit behavioural problems. They are more likely to display positive behaviours and cooperate with others.

- **Self-Control**: Learning to regulate emotions helps children develop self-control and reduce impulsive behaviour.

7. Long-Term Impacts

- **Academic Success**: Emotional regulation and social skills are linked to better academic performance. Children who can manage their emotions are more focused and engaged in learning.

- **Adult Relationships and Success**: Early emotional support sets the stage for healthy adult relationships and professional success. Emotional intelligence, nurtured from a young age, is a key factor in personal and professional life.

3.3 ROLE OF EMOTIONAL SUPPORT IN EARLY CHILDHOOD

3.3.1 The Missing Light

In a quaint village surrounded by rolling hills and blooming meadows, there lived a little girl named Aanya. She had a smile that could brighten the gloomiest days and eyes that sparkled like the morning dew. Aanya was a curious and loving child, always eager to explore the world around her. But beneath her cheerful exterior, she harboured a deep longing for something she couldn't quite name.

Aanya's mother, Meera, was a hardworking woman who juggled multiple jobs to make ends meet. Her father, Raj, was often away for long stretches, working in a distant city. Despite their best efforts, Aanya's parents struggled to provide the emotional support their daughter so desperately needed during her early years.

As Aanya approached her fifth birthday, the lack of emotional nurturing began to take its toll. She became more withdrawn, her voice – never heard, her laughter less frequent, her presence seen often. The village elders, who had watched her grow, noticed the change and worried for her well-being. They knew the importance of a child's formative years and the lasting impact of emotional neglect.

One day, Aanya met an elderly woman named Kamala who lived in a cottage at the edge of the village. Kamala was known for her wisdom and kindness, and the children often visited her for stories and advice. Seeing the sadness in Aanya's eyes, Kamala took her under her wing, offering her the love and attention she was missing. Kamala would tell Aanya stories of brave heroines and magical lands, teaching her about the power of kindness, resilience, and self-worth. Slowly, Aanya began to open up, her laughter returning like a melody lost to time. Yet, despite Kamala's efforts, the wounds of emotional neglect left scars that were not easily healed.

As Aanya grew older, the effects of her early childhood began to manifest in more troubling ways. She struggled with self-esteem, often doubting her worth and abilities. Relationships were challenging as she found it difficult to trust others and express her emotions. The foundation of emotional support she had missed during her first five years cast a long shadow over her life.

But Aanya was not without hope. She carried with her the lessons Kamala had taught, and with time, she began to seek out the support she needed to heal. She joined a community of women who shared their stories and offered each other unwavering support. Through their guidance and her own determination, Aanya embarked on a journey of self-discovery and healing.

Years later, Aanya stood at the village square, sharing her story with a new generation of parents. She spoke of the importance of emotional support in a child's early years and the lasting impact it could have. Her words resonated deeply, inspiring others to prioritise the emotional well-being of their children.

In her childhood, Aanya misses several crucial types of emotional support due to the circumstances her family is in:

Let us delve into the types of Emotional Support Aanya Misses:

3.3.2 The Absence of Affection and Physical Comfort

Missing Components: Regular hugs, kisses, and physical closeness that provide a sense of safety and warmth.

Reason: Her mother, Meera, is often too exhausted from her multiple jobs to spend quality, affectionate time with Aanya. Her father, Raj, is physically absent due to his work in a distant city.

From the moment Aanya was born, she was a bright-eyed child, eager for the world around her. However, as the months turned into years, the subtle signs of neglect began to surface. In the early mornings, when other children were cradled in the arms of their parents, Aanya would often wake up alone. Meera had already left for her job, leaving only a hurriedly prepared breakfast and a note that promised her return.

Aanya's days were spent in the care of various neighbours, none of whom could replace the warmth of a mother's touch. She watched as other children were enveloped in hugs, kissed on the forehead, and held close when they were scared or hurt. These simple acts of affection were a rarity in Aanya's life, and she felt their absence keenly. It had a heavy emotional impact on Aanya which is exhibited as:

1. Sense of Insecurity and Fear:

Without the comforting presence of her parents, Aanya developed a deep-seated sense of insecurity. The world seemed like a vast, unpredictable place, and without the physical reassurance of a hug or a kiss, she felt unanchored.

During thunderstorms or after a bad dream, Aanya would curl up tightly under her blanket, wishing for the warmth and safety that a parent's embrace could provide. The fear she felt in those moments lingered long after the storm had passed or the dream had faded.

2. Difficulty in Expressing Emotions:

The absence of physical affection made it challenging for Aanya to understand and express her own emotions. She often kept her feelings bottled up, unsure of how to seek comfort or share her fears and joys.

She watched other children run to their parents with open arms, receiving comfort and validation. In contrast, Aanya learned to self-soothe, a skill that, while useful, also isolated her emotionally.

3. Impact on Self-Worth:

Physical affection is a powerful affirmation of love and acceptance. Without regular hugs and kisses, Aanya began to doubt her own worth. She wondered if she was less deserving of love, leading to a fragile sense of self-esteem. Simple acts of kindness from strangers or occasional pats on the back from teachers were never enough to fill the void left by her parents' absence.

Aanya developed a deep-seated sense of insecurity due to the lack of consistent affection and physical comfort during her early years. Physical reassurance through hugs, kisses, and gentle touches is crucial for a child's emotional development, providing a tangible sense of safety and trust. For Aanya, these moments of physical affection were rare, creating a significant impact on her emotional well-being. Without regular hugs and kisses, Aanya's world seemed vast and unpredictable. Physical affection from caregivers signals to a child that they are loved, protected, and valued. These acts help anchor a child's emotions, giving them a stable foundation to explore the world. Aanya, deprived of this consistent physical contact, lacked the emotional grounding that helps children feel secure. This absence left her feeling adrift, struggling to find stability in her emotions.

The lack of physical reassurance also made it challenging for Aanya to trust others fully. Trust is built through consistent, positive interactions, including physical affection. Aanya's inconsistent experiences with affection led her to believe that comfort and security were not guaranteed, making her wary and reluctant to rely on others. This wariness extended to her social interactions, where she often felt unworthy of love and attention, making it difficult to form close friendships.

Furthermore, the absence of physical comfort during stressful or frightening moments heightened Aanya's anxiety and fear. During thunderstorms or bad dreams, children often seek the physical presence of their caregivers for reassurance. Without this, Aanya faced her fears alone, amplifying her sense of vulnerability and insecurity.

This heightened anxiety impacted her ability to cope with stress and challenges, leaving her emotionally fragile.

Aanya's lack of early affection also affected her self-esteem. Physical affection is a key component in developing self-worth. Aanya's deprivation led her to internalise feelings of unworthiness, questioning whether she deserved love and affection. This affected her self-image and how she viewed herself in relation to others. She became an overachiever, excelling academically and in other areas, hoping to fill the emotional void. However, these external validations were never enough to compensate for the deep-seated sense of insecurity rooted in her early experiences.

The absence of physical reassurance deprived Aanya of the emotional resilience and sense of belonging that are crucial for a child's development. Regular physical affection fosters a sense of belonging and attachment, reassuring children that they are an important part of their family and community. Aanya's lack of consistent affection left her feeling isolated and disconnected, struggling to find her place in the world. This profound void in her heart affected her perception of her own worth and her sense of belonging, leaving her achievements feeling hollow and her soul yearning for the comfort she missed in her formative years.

In conclusion, Aanya's deep-seated sense of insecurity stemmed from the lack of physical reassurance during her early years. The absence of hugs, kisses, and comforting touches left her feeling unanchored in an unpredictable world. This deprivation impacted her emotional development, leading to difficulties in trust, heightened anxiety, and a constant search for validation. Understanding the critical role of physical affection in a child's development underscores the profound effects of its absence on Aanya's sense of security and well-being.

Moreover, the lack of physical affection impacted Aanya's self-esteem. She internalised the idea that her feelings were not important enough to be noticed or valued. This belief eroded her self-worth and made her doubt her right to express herself. She feared that her emotions were a burden, leading her to suppress them even more.

The absence of physical affection in Aanya's early years significantly hindered her emotional development. She struggled to understand and express her feelings, often keeping them bottled up inside. This emotional isolation prevented her from forming deep connections and affected her self-esteem. While she learned to self-soothe, this skill came at the cost of emotional isolation, reinforcing her belief that she couldn't rely on others for support. Understanding the critical role of physical affection in a child's emotional development highlights the profound effects of its absence on Aanya's ability to navigate her emotional world and build meaningful relationships.

The absence of regular physical affection profoundly impacted Aanya's self-worth. Physical affection, such as hugs and kisses, serves as a powerful affirmation of love and acceptance, helping children feel valued and cherished. Without these consistent gestures from her parents, Aanya began to internalise feelings of doubt about her own worth. She questioned whether she was deserving of love, which eroded her self-esteem and left her with a fragile sense of self. Although she occasionally received simple acts of kindness from strangers or pats on the back from teachers, these moments were fleeting and insufficient to fill the deep void left by her parents' emotional and physical absence. The lack of foundational affection and validation from her primary caregivers left Aanya struggling with persistent feelings of unworthiness, impacting her ability to build a robust and positive self-image.

Withdrawal and isolation became prominent features in Aanya's life due to the absence of regular physical affection and emotional support during her formative years. As a child, Aanya lacked the consistent reassurance of hugs, kisses, and comforting touches from her parents, which are crucial for developing a sense of security and emotional connection. Without these gestures, Aanya struggled to feel safe and valued, leading her to withdraw emotionally and socially.

From an early age, Aanya learned to self-soothe and manage her emotions independently, as the comfort and reassurance she needed were not consistently provided by her caregivers. This self-reliance, while a coping mechanism, also isolated her emotionally from others. Aanya found it difficult to express her feelings openly, unsure of how they would be received or if they were even valid without the validation she needed from her parents.

In social settings, Aanya often felt like an outsider. She observed other children enjoying affectionate interactions with their parents, which reinforced her sense of being different or less deserving. This perception contributed to her withdrawing from social interactions, as she feared rejection or judgement due to her inability to connect emotionally with peers in the same way.

Furthermore, the absence of emotional support impacted Aanya's self-esteem and sense of belonging. She internalised the belief that her emotions were not important enough to be shared or understood, leading to feelings of inadequacy and loneliness. Aanya's withdrawal into herself became a cycle, where the more she felt disconnected, the harder it became to bridge the gap between her internal world and the external environment.

As Aanya grew older, her withdrawal and isolation persisted, affecting her ability to form close relationships and engage fully in social activities. She struggled with trusting others and often felt misunderstood or overlooked, further reinforcing her sense of loneliness and emotional isolation. This pattern of withdrawal not only hindered Aanya's emotional development but also impacted her academic and personal growth, as she missed out on opportunities for peer interaction and emotional support that are vital for holistic development.

In conclusion, Aanya's withdrawal and isolation stemmed from the lack of regular physical affection and emotional support during her childhood. Addressing these emotional needs through consistent love, affirmation, and support could have helped Aanya feel more secure, valued, and connected to others. Understanding the profound impact of early emotional experiences underscores the importance of nurturing emotional bonds and providing a supportive environment for children's healthy development.

What Could Have Been Done?

To address Aanya's deep-seated sense of insecurity, her parents, Meera and Raj, could have made concerted efforts to provide a stable, nurturing environment rich in physical affection and emotional support. Regular, consistent acts of physical affection, such as hugs and kisses, would have helped ground her emotions and provide a sense of safety. Setting aside dedicated quality time each day for engaging activities and open communication would have made Aanya feel valued and understood, reinforcing her emotional connection with her parents. Building a broader support network with extended family and trusted friends could have offered additional sources of comfort and validation. Acknowledging and validating Aanya's feelings through empathetic communication would have encouraged her to express her emotions freely. Positive reinforcement and praise for her efforts and achievements would boost her self-esteem and counter feelings of unworthiness. Establishing a predictable routine would have provided the stability she needed to feel secure. Professional counselling could have offered specialised support to address her emotional challenges, and ensuring that her parents also took care of their own emotional well-being would enable them to be more present and supportive. These combined efforts would help Aanya develop a stronger sense of security and self-worth.

To address Aanya's lack of physical affection and emotional support, her parents, Meera and Raj, could have incorporated more physical affection into daily interactions, such as hugs, kisses, and holding hands, to provide reassurance and security. They could have set aside quality time each day for focused attention and emotional check-ins, building a stronger bond through shared activities like reading and playing. Involving extended family or trusted neighbours could have created a supportive network to compensate for their absence. Acknowledging and validating Aanya's feelings, offering praise and positive reinforcement, and establishing a predictable routine would have further contributed to her emotional stability. Seeking professional counselling could provide additional support and strategies for both Aanya and her parents. By also managing their own stress and ensuring their well-being, Meera and Raj would be better equipped to provide the necessary affection and emotional nurturing that Aanya needed for a secure and happy childhood.

To address Aanya's fragile self-worth, her parents, Meera and Raj, could have implemented several strategies to provide consistent love and affirmation. Regular physical affection, such as daily hugs, kisses, and gentle touches, would affirm her value and importance, helping to build her self-esteem. Spending quality time together, engaging in meaningful conversations, and showing interest in her activities and feelings would reinforce her sense of being valued and understood. Providing verbal affirmations and praise for her efforts and achievements, no matter how small, would help counter feelings of doubt and boost her confidence. Building a supportive environment with extended family and friends who could offer additional encouragement and love would also be beneficial. Ensuring that Aanya's emotional needs were consistently met through active listening and empathetic responses would help her develop a positive self-image. If needed, seeking professional counselling could provide specialised support and strategies for bolstering her self-esteem. By addressing her emotional needs with love, attention, and affirmation, Aanya's parents could help her develop a strong, healthy sense of self-worth.

3.3.3 Behavioural Changes and Coping Mechanisms

As Aanya grew older, the lack of affection manifested in various ways:

1. Withdrawal and Isolation:

Aanya became more withdrawn, often preferring solitude over playdates and social interactions. She found comfort in books and imaginary friends, creating a safe space where she felt loved and understood.

2. Overachievement and Perfectionism:

In an unconscious attempt to earn the affection she craved, Aanya became an overachiever. She excelled academically, hoping that her accomplishments would draw her parents' attention and love.

The constant drive for perfection, however, only added to her stress and anxiety, as no amount of success seemed to fill the emotional void.

3. Longing for Connection:

Despite her withdrawal, Aanya's longing for connection was evident. She often lingered around affectionate families, observing their interactions with a mix of admiration and envy.

She would volunteer to help neighbours with their chores, not just out of kindness, but in the hope of receiving a warm smile or a gentle touch as a reward.

Aanya's overachievement and perfectionism stemmed from a deep-seated desire to earn the affection and attention she lacked due to the absence of regular physical affection and emotional support from her parents, Meera and Raj. Excelling academically became her primary way of seeking validation, hoping that her accomplishments would finally draw her parents' attention and love. However, the constant pursuit of perfection only intensified her stress and anxiety. Despite her academic successes, Aanya found that no amount of achievement could fill the emotional void left by the lack of nurturing and affection in her early years. The pressure to constantly excel took a toll on her mental and emotional well-being, reinforcing her belief that her worth was tied solely to her achievements. This cycle of overachievement and perfectionism became a double-edged sword, driving her to strive for external validation while deepening her sense of inadequacy and emotional longing.

Aanya's longing for connection stemmed from the profound emotional void left by the absence of regular physical affection and emotional support in her early years. Without consistent hugs, kisses, and reassuring touches from her parents, Meera and Raj, Aanya felt a deep yearning for emotional closeness and validation. She observed other children enjoying affectionate interactions with their parents, which highlighted her own sense of isolation and longing. This longing extended beyond just physical touch; Aanya craved meaningful emotional connections where she could feel understood, valued, and accepted for who she truly was. However, lacking these foundational experiences of emotional nurturing made it challenging for her to trust others and open up about her feelings. As a result, Aanya often felt disconnected from her peers and struggled to form deep, meaningful relationships. Her longing for connection underscored her innate need for emotional security and validation, shaping her emotional development and influencing how she perceived herself and others in her life. Addressing this longing required nurturing her emotional well-being through consistent love, empathy, and support to help Aanya build trust, feel emotionally secure, and cultivate healthy relationships in her life.

To address Aanya's overachievement and perfectionism driven by her need for parental affection, Meera and Raj should prioritise nurturing her emotional well-being over solely emphasising academic success. They can start by actively listening to Aanya's feelings and validating her emotions, emphasising that her value is inherent and not solely dependent on achievements. Encouraging a balanced approach to life where Aanya can explore hobbies, interests, and social activities will help alleviate the pressure to constantly excel academically. Setting realistic expectations and celebrating effort rather than just outcomes will foster a growth-oriented mindset and reduce anxiety. Meera and Raj should also model self-compassion and resilience in their own behaviour, demonstrating that mistakes are opportunities for learning and growth. Seeking guidance from a counsellor or psychologist specialising in adolescent development can provide additional tools and strategies to support Aanya in managing perfectionism and building healthy self-esteem.

3.3.4 Succeeding out of Fearful Pain

I personally feel it is such a pathetic condition that a child has to undergo deprival of the basic love and attention which is abundantly given by nature. The emotional and psychological impact on a child deprived of basic love and attention is profound. Anaya's condition is indeed tragic, reflecting a profound deprivation of the basic love and attention that are naturally provided by a nurturing environment. In everything she does, everything she sees, and everything she comes in contact with—physically, emotionally, or mentally—the absence of affection casts a long shadow.

Despite being a hero in her own life, leading a solitary path with remarkable resilience, and achieving outstanding grades and accolades, Anaya's journey is bittersweet. She excels in ways that other children and their parents can only dream of, yet the core of her heart remains filled with a persistent sense of insecurity. Her accomplishments, which should be celebrated, are overshadowed by a deep, lingering emptiness. While other children revel in their successes and the loving support of their families, Anaya feels a vast vacuum within her. Her journey, remarkable as it is, lacks the foundational emotional security that can only come from consistent love and affection. This profound void in her heart affects her perception of her own worth and her sense of belonging, leaving her achievements feeling hollow and her soul yearning for the comfort she missed in her formative years.

The absence of physical affection profoundly impacted Aanya's ability to understand and express her emotions. In her early years, physical affection plays a crucial role in helping children learn to identify, manage, and communicate their feelings. For Aanya, the lack of regular hugs, kisses, and comforting touches left her emotionally adrift. Without these tangible reassurances, she struggled to make sense of her emotions and often felt overwhelmed by them. Aanya found it challenging to articulate her feelings, both positive and negative. When she was happy or excited, she didn't know how to share her joy with others. When she was sad, scared, or anxious, she didn't have the words or the confidence to seek comfort from those around her. This inability to express her emotions led to a habit of bottling them up inside. She kept her fears, frustrations, and even her happiness to herself, creating an emotional barrier that distanced her from others.

She often observed other children running to their parents with open arms, easily receiving comfort and validation. She saw how they were held, soothed, and reassured, learning from these interactions that their feelings were important and worthy of attention. In contrast, Aanya didn't have this model of emotional support. Instead, she learned to self-soothe—a skill that, while beneficial in certain situations, also led to emotional isolation. Self-soothing allowed her to manage her immediate distress, but it reinforced the notion that she couldn't rely on others for support.

This self-reliance in managing her emotions made it difficult for Aanya to build deep, trusting relationships. She found it hard to open up to others, fearing that her feelings might be dismissed or misunderstood. This fear of rejection or invalidation kept her from seeking the comfort and connection she needed. Instead of reaching out, she retreated further into herself, creating a cycle of emotional isolation.

Aanya's inability to express her emotions also affected her interactions with peers and adults. She appeared reserved and distant, leading others to perceive her as aloof or uninterested. This misperception further isolated her, as potential friends and supporters didn't understand her internal struggle. In social situations, Aanya often felt like an outsider, unable to bridge the gap between her internal world and the external environment.

To address Aanya's longing for connection stemming from the lack of emotional nurturing, Meera and Raj should prioritise creating a nurturing environment centred on empathy and understanding. They can start by actively listening to Aanya's feelings and validating her emotions, reassuring her that she is valued and loved unconditionally. Dedicate quality time regularly for bonding activities that Aanya enjoys, fostering deeper connections through shared experiences and meaningful conversations. Encouraging Aanya's social interactions with peers and providing opportunities for her to build friendships in supportive settings will help alleviate feelings of isolation. It's also crucial to model healthy relationships within the family, demonstrating effective communication and empathy. Seeking guidance from a child psychologist or counsellor specialising in emotional development can offer additional support and strategies tailored to Aanya's needs. By consistently nurturing her emotional well-being and building trust, Meera and Raj can help Aanya develop the connections and sense of belonging she longs for, fostering her overall happiness and resilience.

Turning Point

The turning point came when Aanya met Kamala, the elderly woman at the edge of the village. Kamala's cottage was filled with warmth, both in its physical cosiness and in the affection she showered upon Aanya. Kamala made it a point to hug Aanya when she arrived, pat her back encouragingly during their storytelling sessions, and kiss her forehead goodnight when she left.

Through Kamala's love, Aanya began to experience the physical comfort she had missed. The simple acts of holding hands while walking or being hugged tightly when she was sad slowly mended the broken pieces of her heart. Kamala's consistent affection provided a safe haven for Aanya, allowing her to open up emotionally and build the self-worth that had been eroded over the years.

CONCLUSION

Attention and Presence

Missed: Being listened to, having her thoughts and feelings acknowledged, and spending one-on-one time with her parents.

Reason: Meera's busy schedule leaves little time for focused attention on Aanya. Raj's absence means fewer opportunities for father-daughter bonding moments.

Emotional Validation:

Missed: Receiving reassurance, empathy, and understanding of her emotions and experiences.

Reason: Meera, overwhelmed by her responsibilities, might unintentionally dismiss or overlook Aanya's emotional needs. Raj's infrequent visits make it difficult for him to be in tune with Aanya's emotional state.

Guidance and Encouragement:

Missed: Encouraging words, positive reinforcement, and support in her endeavours.

Reason: Meera's focus on survival and providing for basic needs can overshadow the importance of nurturing Aanya's interests and self-esteem. Raj's limited presence means fewer opportunities to guide and encourage her.

Security and Stability:

Missed: Consistent routines and the feeling of a stable, predictable environment.

Reason: The economic struggles and Meera's multiple jobs create an unpredictable and often chaotic home environment. Raj's absence contributes to a sense of instability.

The absence of attention, emotional validation, guidance, and stability in Aanya's life has created a gap in her emotional and psychological development, highlighting the critical role of these foundational elements in a child's growth. Aanya's unmet needs for focused attention, reassurance, and encouragement, as well as her desire for a stable environment, shape not only her sense of self-worth but also her ability to trust in the consistency of relationships around her. When children like Aanya do not receive consistent acknowledgement and validation, they may begin to internalise feelings of being unworthy or invisible, leading to self-doubt and insecurity. The lack of one-on-one time with her parents, especially due to Meera's demanding schedule and Raj's absence, means that Aanya misses out on crucial bonding moments that build trust, empathy, and open communication. Emotional validation, often communicated through simple acts of listening and empathy, reassures children that their feelings matter and are understood. For Aanya, however, Meera's overwhelming responsibilities and Raj's infrequent presence may inadvertently lead to her emotional needs being overlooked, causing Aanya to feel isolated in her experiences and possibly misunderstood.

Similarly, guidance and encouragement are vital in fostering a child's confidence, curiosity, and self-esteem. Without regular, positive reinforcement, Aanya may lack the motivation and self-assurance to pursue her interests, which could impact her later in life by limiting her confidence in her abilities. Guidance from both parents offers a balanced perspective, but Raj's absence means that she misses out on this valuable support, making her feel less certain about her choices and potential. Furthermore, the unpredictability of Aanya's home environment, caused by Meera's economic struggles and multiple jobs, deprives her of a sense of security and stability that is crucial during her formative years. Stability offers a child reassurance and a solid foundation to explore, learn, and grow. Without it, Aanya may develop heightened anxiety or fear of change, as her day-to-day life lacks the comfort of routine and consistency.

In summary, the absence of these key elements creates a profound void in Aanya's development. Children flourish when they are given attention, validation, guidance, and stability, and the absence of these factors can leave them feeling uncertain, unsupported, and vulnerable. The challenge here underscores the importance of parental presence—not just in fulfilling material needs but in offering emotional support, structure, and encouragement that allow a child to grow into a confident and secure individual. Without this foundation, Aanya's sense of self and her ability to form healthy relationships in the future may be compromised. This scenario serves as a reminder of how essential it is for caregivers to balance life's demands with the emotional needs of their children, as these formative experiences will have lasting impacts on their resilience, self-image, and emotional health.

Reasons for Missing Emotional Support:

Economic Hardship: Meera's need to work multiple jobs to support the family financially limits the time and energy she can devote to Aanya.

Parental Absence: Raj's job in a distant city means he is physically absent for extended periods, reducing his ability to provide emotional support.

Stress and Exhaustion: The stress and exhaustion from Meera's demanding schedule make it difficult for her to be emotionally available and responsive to Aanya's needs.

Lack of Community Support: Without a strong support system or extended family nearby, Meera has little help in balancing work and parenting responsibilities.

The lack of emotional support in Aanya's life can be traced to a combination of economic hardship, parental absence, stress, and insufficient community support, all of which place a heavy strain on her mother, Meera. The family's financial struggles have forced Meera into the demanding position of working multiple jobs, which consumes her time and energy, leaving little room for one-on-one interaction with Aanya. This constant work schedule may fulfill the family's basic material needs but inadvertently limits Meera's availability to provide the emotional nurturing that Aanya requires. Compounding this, Aanya's father, Raj, works in a distant city and is often physically absent for extended periods. This separation reduces his involvement in daily parenting, making it difficult for him to form a close, consistent bond with Aanya or provide the paternal support she needs. Meera, already overwhelmed by financial pressures, faces additional stress and exhaustion, which can affect her emotional presence. This fatigue can make it challenging for her to respond empathetically to Aanya's emotional needs, often leading to unintentional neglect of the little gestures that foster security and validation in a child. Moreover, the absence of extended family or a local support network means Meera lacks the assistance needed to balance her work and parenting responsibilities. Without a community to lean on, Meera faces these burdens largely alone, which amplifies the stress on her and reduces her ability to offer the emotional support that is essential for Aanya's development. This combination of factors highlights the importance of support systems—both within the family and the broader community—in providing children with the nurturing they need to thrive emotionally.

3.4 EMOTIONAL MILESTONES IN MIDDLE CHILDHOOD

Middle childhood, spanning ages 6 to 12, is a crucial period for emotional development, marked by significant growth in understanding and expressing emotions, developing self-esteem, forming complex friendships, and deepening empathy and moral understanding. Children in this stage seek more independence, learn to cope with stress and anxiety, and build resilience through overcoming challenges. They become more aware of social roles and expectations, shaping their self-concept and social interactions. Providing a supportive and nurturing environment with positive reinforcement from parents, teachers, and peers is essential for fostering healthy emotional development during this formative period. At age 6, children often face difficulties in expressing emotions due to limited vocabulary and understanding of complex feelings, which can lead to frustration and behavioural issues.

To support their children, parents should model healthy emotional expression and create a safe environment for open communication. Teaching an emotional vocabulary helps children articulate their feelings more accurately. Parents should validate their child's emotions, acknowledging them as normal and important, while providing coping strategies like deep breathing or drawing. Reading books and telling stories about emotions can also aid understanding, and consistent emotional support and reassurance are essential for helping children navigate their emotional experiences.

At age 6, children may struggle with developing self-esteem, forming complex friendships, and deepening empathy and moral understanding. These challenges arise as they begin comparing themselves to others, which can lead to feelings of inadequacy and impact self-esteem. Forming friendships becomes more complex as they must navigate social dynamics and conflicts, and their understanding of empathy and morality is still developing, making it difficult to fully grasp others' perspectives. Parents play a crucial role in supporting their children through these challenges by providing positive reinforcement to boost self-esteem, guiding them in resolving conflicts and fostering friendships, and modelling empathetic and moral behaviour. Consistent encouragement, open communication, and teaching by example help children build confidence, form meaningful relationships, and develop a strong sense of empathy and morality.

3.4.1 Developing Self-Esteem at Age 6

At age 6, children are at a critical juncture in their development, and their self-esteem can be particularly vulnerable. This is an age where they start school, which introduces them to a broader social environment and new challenges. They begin to compare themselves to their peers in areas such as academics, athletics, and social skills. These comparisons can impact their self-perception positively or negatively. At the age of six, children are in a pivotal stage of social and emotional development, as they begin to establish their sense of self-esteem, navigate complex friendships, and deepen their empathy and moral understanding. Parents play an instrumental role in guiding children through these developmental milestones by fostering a supportive, empathetic environment and providing consistent encouragement, modelling, and reinforcement of positive behaviours. Each of these milestones presents its own challenges and requires a thoughtful approach to help children grow into confident, compassionate individuals.

Self-esteem at this age is closely linked to the feedback children receive from their environment. Entering formal schooling introduces them to a new social structure where they often compare themselves to peers in academics, sports, and social interactions. Struggles with self-esteem can arise from academic pressures, peer comparisons, adult feedback, peer relationships, and family dynamics. Academic struggles can lead to self-doubt if children perceive they aren't meeting expectations, while comparisons with peers can create feelings of inferiority when they see others excelling in areas where they feel less capable. Additionally, negative feedback from adults can chip away at a child's confidence, while positive reinforcement can strengthen it. Similarly, difficulties in forming friendships or feeling excluded by peers can impact a child's self-worth. Family dynamics, too, shape self-esteem, with supportive, loving environments fostering confidence, while critical or stressful home situations may undermine it.

To support self-esteem, parents can provide positive reinforcement by acknowledging a child's efforts and achievements, thus helping them build confidence. Encouraging resilience through the message that mistakes are learning opportunities enables children to accept challenges without fear of failure. By modelling self-confidence and self-compassion, parents offer children a positive example of self-worth. Creating a safe, loving home environment where children feel valued establishes a stable foundation for healthy self-esteem, while teaching problem-solving skills allows them to feel capable and empowered in handling situations independently. Together, these practices help children approach challenges with a positive mindset and lay the groundwork for a strong sense of self-worth.

Struggles with Self-Esteem

Struggles with self-esteem at this age can stem from various sources:

1. Academic Pressure:

Entering a formal educational setting can be overwhelming. If children struggle with schoolwork or feel they are not meeting expectations, they may start to doubt their abilities. The pressure to perform well academically can lead to stress and a sense of inadequacy if they perceive themselves as failing to meet the standards set by teachers or parents.

2. Social Comparisons:

Children notice differences between themselves and their peers in terms of skills, appearance, and possessions. This awareness can lead to feelings of inferiority if they perceive themselves as lacking in any area. For example, seeing a peer excel in sports or receive praise for academic achievements might make a child feel less capable or valuable.

3. Feedback from Adults:

The feedback children receive from parents, teachers, and other adults plays a significant role in shaping their self-esteem. Negative or overly critical comments can damage a child's self-confidence, while positive reinforcement can boost it. Constructive feedback is essential to help children understand that making mistakes is part of learning and growing.

4. Peer Relationships:

Forming friendships and fitting in with peers is crucial at this age. Difficulties in making friends or experiencing rejection can negatively affect a child's self-worth. Children are highly sensitive to social dynamics and can feel deeply hurt by exclusion or bullying.

5. Family Dynamics:

The home environment significantly impacts a child's self-esteem. Supportive, loving families typically foster higher self-esteem, while stressful or critical family dynamics can undermine it. Consistent emotional support from family members helps children feel valued and understood.

The Role of Parents

Parents play a crucial role in helping their children develop healthy self-esteem:

- **Positive Reinforcement:** Regularly acknowledging and celebrating a child's efforts and achievements, no matter how small, helps build confidence. Simple praises like "You did a great job" or "I'm proud of you" can make a significant difference.

- **Encouragement and Support:** Encouraging children to try new things and reassuring them when they face challenges or failures teaches resilience and self-acceptance. Letting them know it's okay to make mistakes helps them learn and grow without fear of failure.

- **Modelling Positive Self-Esteem:** Demonstrating self-confidence and self-compassion in their behaviour provides children with a positive example to emulate. Children often imitate the behaviour of adults, so displaying a healthy self-image and positive attitude is crucial.

- **Creating a Safe Environment:** Providing a loving and secure home environment where children feel valued and accepted helps them develop a strong sense of self-worth. Consistent routines and clear expectations contribute to a sense of stability and security.

- **Teaching Problem-Solving Skills:** Helping children develop problem-solving skills and autonomy boosts their confidence in their abilities to handle different situations. Encouraging them to think of solutions to problems they encounter fosters independence and self-assurance.

By understanding the challenges and providing consistent support, parents can help their children navigate this critical stage of development and build a healthy, positive self-esteem. Creating an environment where children feel safe, loved, and capable sets the foundation for their overall well-being and future success.

3.4.2 Forming Complex Friendships at Age 6

At age 6, children begin to develop more complex friendships as they move beyond simple playmates to form deeper, more meaningful relationships. This stage of social development is marked by an increased ability to understand others' feelings, engage in cooperative play, and navigate the social dynamics of larger groups. Friendships at this age become more intricate as children begin to understand others' feelings and participate in cooperative play. However, this deepening social engagement brings its own challenges. Children may feel overwhelmed by social hierarchies and dynamics, experience difficulties in resolving conflicts, and struggle with empathy and perspective-taking. As they become more aware of group dynamics, they might feel excluded or competitive, and they are still learning the skills needed to handle disagreements effectively. Peer pressure also begins to emerge as children seek acceptance, sometimes prompting them to act in ways that conflict with their own preferences. Additionally, inclusion and exclusion become prominent issues, with children experiencing the impact of social acceptance or rejection on their self-esteem.

Parents can play a key role in helping their children navigate these challenges. By modelling social skills like active listening and empathy, parents provide a practical example for their children. Facilitating supervised playdates allows children to practice these skills in a safe environment. Teaching emotional intelligence by helping children recognise and understand emotions fosters empathy and improves their ability to connect with peers. Encouraging diverse friendships expands children's social skills and reduces the likelihood of exclusion. Guiding children through conflict resolution empowers them to manage disputes constructively. Finally, promoting positive self-esteem enables children to approach social interactions with confidence, making them more resilient in social settings. Through these actions, parents support their children's journey to build lasting, positive friendships that will benefit them throughout their lives.

Struggles with Forming Complex Friendships

1. Navigating Social Dynamics:

Children at this age start to understand social hierarchies and group dynamics. They become more aware of status and popularity, which can lead to feelings of exclusion or competition. Understanding how to fit into these dynamics can be challenging and sometimes overwhelming.

2.Conflict Resolution:

As friendships deepen, conflicts are inevitable. Six-year-olds are still developing the skills needed to resolve disagreements effectively. They may struggle with expressing their feelings, listening to others, and finding fair solutions.

3. Empathy and Perspective-Taking:

While children are becoming more empathetic, they are still learning to see things from another's perspective fully. This can make it difficult for them to understand their friends' needs and feelings, leading to misunderstandings and conflicts.

4. Peer Pressure:

Children begin to experience peer pressure, wanting to fit in with their friends and avoid rejection. This can sometimes lead them to behave in ways that are out of character or uncomfortable for them, creating internal conflicts.

5. Inclusion and Exclusion:

Issues of inclusion and exclusion become more prominent. Children may experience the pain of being left out or the dilemma of whether to include others in their established groups. These experiences can significantly impact their self-esteem and social confidence.

The Role of Parents

Parents play a crucial role in helping their children navigate these complexities and form healthy, positive friendships:

- **Modelling Social Skills:** Demonstrating effective social skills, such as active listening, empathy, and conflict resolution, provides children with a practical blueprint for their interactions. Parents can model these behaviours in their interactions with others and through role-playing activities with their children.

- **Facilitating Playdates:** Organising and supervising playdates allows children to practice their social skills in a safe, controlled environment. Parents can gently guide interactions, helping children navigate conflicts and encouraging inclusive play.

- **Teaching Emotional Intelligence:** Helping children recognise and label their emotions, as well as understand the emotions of others, fosters empathy and improves their ability to connect with peers. Discussing emotions openly and validating children's feelings are key strategies.

- **Encouraging Diverse Friendships:** Encouraging children to form friendships with a diverse group of peers helps them learn to appreciate different perspectives and reduces the likelihood of exclusion. Parents can introduce their children to various social settings and activities.

- **Providing Guidance on Conflict Resolution:** Teaching children how to resolve conflicts constructively is crucial. Parents can role-play scenarios, provide language for expressing feelings and needs, and coach children on finding fair solutions.

- **Promoting Positive Self-Esteem:** Reinforcing a child's self-worth and confidence helps them approach social interactions with a positive mindset. Parents can do this by praising their child's efforts in social situations, encouraging them to try again after setbacks, and supporting their interests and activities.

- **Monitoring Social Interactions:** Keeping an eye on their child's social interactions and stepping in when necessary can prevent negative patterns from developing. Parents should be observant and ready to offer guidance without being overly intrusive.

By actively supporting their child's social development, parents can help them form complex, rewarding friendships. This foundation of social skills and emotional intelligence will benefit children throughout their lives, enabling them to build healthy, positive relationships.

3.4.3 Deepening Empathy and Moral Understanding at Age 6

At age 6, children begin to develop a more profound sense of empathy and moral understanding. They start to grasp the concept of right and wrong more clearly and become more capable of understanding and sharing the feelings of others. However, this development comes with its own set of challenges. As children's cognitive abilities expand, so does their capacity for empathy and moral reasoning. At this age, children begin to grasp concepts of right and wrong, understand the importance of kindness, and become more capable of recognising and sharing others' feelings. However, understanding complex emotions, perspective-taking, moral reasoning, and conflict resolution still pose challenges. Children may struggle to interpret subtle emotions and see things from another's viewpoint, especially when emotions are contradictory. Their moral reasoning is often black-and-white, and they may have difficulty applying empathy during conflicts, focusing instead on their own needs. The influence of external factors, such as family values, school culture, media, and peer behaviours, further complicates their understanding of empathy and morality.

Parents can nurture empathy and moral development through multiple approaches. Modelling empathy and ethical behaviour in daily life provides children with an example to follow. Open discussions about feelings and moral dilemmas help children understand complex emotions and ethical choices, encouraging them to think critically about right and wrong. Encouraging perspective-taking by asking children to consider others' viewpoints fosters empathy. Reinforcing positive behaviour with praise encourages children to repeat compassionate actions. Providing diverse experiences helps children appreciate different perspectives, while teaching conflict resolution equips them with tools to apply empathy in real-life interactions. Clear expectations about behaviour reinforce boundaries and explain the importance of empathy and fairness, while reading stories with moral lessons deepens children's understanding of ethical choices and compassion.

Challenges in Deepening Empathy and Moral Understanding

1. Understanding Complex Emotions:

While six-year-olds are becoming better at recognising basic emotions, understanding complex or mixed emotions can be challenging. They might struggle to identify why someone feels a certain way, especially if the emotions are subtle or contradictory.

2. Perspective-Taking:

Developing the ability to see things from another person's perspective is a critical component of empathy. However, at this age, children are still learning to move beyond their own viewpoint to fully appreciate someone else's feelings and experiences.

3. Moral Reasoning:

Six-year-olds are beginning to understand the reasons behind rules and the concept of fairness, but their moral reasoning is still relatively black-and-white. They may have difficulty understanding more nuanced ethical dilemmas and the idea that different situations might require different moral considerations.

4. Handling Conflicts:

Empathy and moral understanding are crucial in resolving conflicts, but children at this age might find it hard to apply these concepts in practice. They may struggle with balancing their own needs and desires with those of others during disputes.

5. Influence of External Factors:

Children are influenced by their environment, including family, school, media, and peers. Inconsistent messages from these sources can confuse their developing sense of empathy and morality. Parental Support for Deepening Empathy and Moral Understanding.

Parents play a pivotal role in nurturing their child's empathy and moral development. Here are some ways they can provide support:

1. **Modelling Empathy and Morality:** Children learn a great deal by observing their parents' behaviour. Demonstrating empathy and ethical behaviour in everyday interactions provides a powerful example for children to follow. Parents should show kindness, fairness, and understanding in their actions and words.

2. **Open Discussions:** Engaging in open discussions about feelings and moral dilemmas helps children understand these concepts better. Parents can use stories, real-life situations, and hypothetical scenarios to discuss emotions and moral choices, asking questions like, "How do you think she felt?" or "What would be the right thing to do here?"

3. **Encouraging Perspective-Taking:** Activities that encourage children to consider others' perspectives can deepen their empathy. Parents can ask their children to imagine how others might feel in various situations and discuss why they might feel that way.

4. **Reinforcing Positive Behaviour:** Praising and reinforcing empathetic and moral behaviour when it occurs encourages

children to continue acting in these ways. Positive reinforcement helps children understand the value of their actions and motivates them to repeat them.

5. **Providing Diverse Experiences:** Exposing children to diverse environments and people helps them understand different perspectives and cultures, fostering a broader sense of empathy and fairness. Parents can encourage interactions with a wide range of individuals and participate in community activities that promote inclusivity.

6. **Teaching Conflict Resolution:** Guiding children through conflict resolution processes helps them apply empathy and moral reasoning in real-life situations. Parents can teach children to express their feelings, listen to others, and find mutually acceptable solutions to disputes.

7. **Setting Clear Expectations:** Clear and consistent expectations about behaviour help children understand the boundaries of acceptable conduct. Parents should explain the reasons behind rules and the importance of empathy and fairness in their family and community.

8. **Reading and Storytelling:** Reading books and telling stories that involve moral lessons and empathetic characters can help children internalise these values. Parents can choose stories that illustrate the importance of understanding others and making ethical choices.

By actively engaging in these practices, parents can significantly support their child's journey towards deeper empathy and moral understanding, laying a foundation for their social and emotional growth.

In sum, parents are pivotal guides in helping children navigate this stage of growth. Through active involvement, they lay the foundation for their child's emotional intelligence, social skills, and moral reasoning. By fostering a safe, supportive environment and modelling positive behaviours, parents equip children with the tools they need to form a resilient self-esteem, build meaningful friendships, and develop empathy and a sense of morality. These skills will not only benefit children in their early years but will also serve as cornerstones of their social and emotional lives, enabling them to build healthy relationships and contribute positively to their communities in the future.

3.5 ADOLESCENT EMOTIONAL DEVELOPMENT.

Adolescent emotional development is a crucial phase in a person's life where they undergo significant changes in how they understand and manage their emotions. This stage, which typically spans from around ages 10 to 19, involves several key aspects:

1. **Identity Formation**: Adolescents begin to explore their own identity and self-concept. This involves questioning who they are, what they believe, and where they fit in socially. Emotional experiences during this period are often intense as they work to establish their own identity separate from their parents or caregivers.

2. **Emotional Regulation**: Teens develop more sophisticated ways to manage and express their emotions. This can include learning to control impulsive reactions, understanding complex emotions, and developing coping strategies for stress and anxiety.

3. **Empathy and Perspective-Taking**: The ability to understand and share the feelings of others grows during adolescence.

This enhanced empathy helps improve social relationships and contributes to more nuanced emotional responses.

4. **Self-Esteem and Body Image**: Adolescents are highly sensitive to their self-image and how they are perceived by others. Changes in their physical appearance and social feedback can significantly impact their self-esteem and emotional well-being.

5. **Social Relationships**: Peer relationships become more central to emotional development. Adolescents often seek validation and support from their peers, which can influence their self-worth and emotional state.

6. **Emotional Intensity**: Emotions during adolescence can be more intense and fluctuating due to hormonal changes and the ongoing development of the brain's emotional regulation systems.

7. **Decision-Making and Risk-Taking**: Emotional development also affects decision-making processes. Adolescents may engage in risk-taking behaviours as they test boundaries and explore their independence.

Supporting adolescents through this developmental stage involves providing a stable and understanding environment, fostering open communication, and helping them develop healthy coping mechanisms for managing their emotions.

Adolescent emotional development is deeply intertwined with the influence of opposite-sex relationships and the challenges of decision-making. Here's a closer look at these aspects:

3.5.1 Influence of Opposite-Sex on Adolescent Emotional Development

1. **Romantic Interests**: Romantic feelings and relationships become significant during adolescence. These relationships can impact self-esteem, emotional security, and social dynamics. Adolescents may experience intense emotions related to attraction, love, and rejection, which can contribute to their overall emotional growth.

2. **Social and Peer Pressure**: The presence of opposite-sex peers often introduces social pressures and expectations. Adolescents might feel compelled to conform to certain behaviours or attitudes, which can affect their emotional well-being and self-perception.

3. **Emotional Intensity**: Interactions with the opposite-sex can amplify emotional experiences. First crushes, dating, and breakups can lead to heightened emotional responses, which can be both challenging and formative for emotional development.

4. **Identity and Self-Concept**: Relationships with the opposite-sex can play a role in shaping adolescents' sense of identity. These interactions might influence how they see themselves and their role in relationships, affecting their overall self-concept.

3.5.2 Challenges Faced During Adolescent Emotional Development

1. **Self-Esteem Issues**: Adolescents are often concerned with their self-image and how they are perceived by others, including those of the opposite-sex. This can lead to fluctuations in self-esteem and emotional distress.

2. **Emotional Regulation**: The ability to manage intense emotions and stress can be challenging. Adolescents might struggle with mood swings, impulsivity, and difficulty in regulating their emotions, especially in the context of romantic relationships.

3. **Conflicting Emotions**: The transition from childhood to adulthood brings a mix of conflicting emotions, such as excitement and anxiety about new experiences and relationships. Navigating these conflicting feelings can be difficult.

4. **Pressure to Conform**: Adolescents may feel pressured to meet societal or peer expectations, particularly in their interactions with the opposite-sex. This pressure can lead to stress and emotional confusion.

3.5.3 Ambiguity in Decision-Making

1. **Uncertainty**: Adolescents often face uncertainty in decision-making due to a lack of experience and a developing ability to weigh long-term consequences. This ambiguity can lead to indecision and stress.

2. **Influence of Peers**: Peer opinions can heavily influence decisions, especially regarding relationships and social behaviour. Adolescents might struggle to balance their own preferences with peer pressure.

3. **Balancing Independence and Dependence**: Adolescents are learning to make independent decisions while still relying on parental guidance. Striking this balance can be challenging and can contribute to feelings of ambiguity.

4. **Future Planning**: Decisions about future goals, such as career aspirations and educational choices, can be overwhelming. The uncertainty about the future can impact emotional well-being and decision-making.

Support during this period involves providing guidance, fostering open communication, and helping adolescents develop skills for emotional regulation and decision-making. Encouraging self-reflection and resilience can also aid them in navigating these complex emotional and social landscapes. Adolescence is a transformative stage marked by intense emotional and social challenges as individuals navigate self-discovery, social dynamics, and increasing independence. Self-esteem often fluctuates as adolescents become more aware of their appearance, behaviour, and social standing, frequently comparing themselves to peers and worrying about how others, especially the opposite-sex, perceive them. This focus on self-image, coupled with new experiences like romantic attraction, can make them sensitive to feedback, leading to heightened self-doubt or, alternatively, confidence when reassured by positive attention. Another challenge adolescents face is emotional regulation. The hormonal and neurological changes during this period can intensify emotions, making it difficult for them to manage mood swings and impulses. In romantic contexts, these challenges are heightened, as emotions like excitement, fear, and disappointment can feel overwhelming, often resulting in impulsive behaviours or conflicts in relationships.

Conflicting emotions also become prevalent as adolescents transition from childhood to adulthood. They may feel both excitement and anxiety about growing up, handling new responsibilities, and exploring relationships. Adolescents are drawn to new experiences but often grapple with the fear of failure, leading to internal conflict. At the same time, societal and peer pressures encourage them to conform to specific expectations about behaviour, looks, and interests, adding to their stress. This pressure to fit in can create emotional confusion as they try to align with group norms while exploring their individuality.

Ambiguity in decision-making is also a defining feature of adolescence. Faced with choices about friendships, romantic interests, and career aspirations, they often struggle due to a lack of experience and underdeveloped long-term planning skills. The influence of peers significantly impacts their decision-making, especially in social and relationship contexts. Balancing the desire for independence with parental guidance can also be complex, as they seek autonomy but often still need support. Planning for the future, including education and career paths, can be intimidating, contributing to feelings of stress and doubt about their choices. During this time, consistent support and guidance from parents, mentors, and friends are vital, helping adolescents manage their emotions, develop decision-making skills, and foster self-awareness. By encouraging open communication, resilience, and self-reflection, adults can assist adolescents in navigating this intricate emotional landscape, ultimately supporting their journey toward emotional maturity and personal growth.

Adolescents may experience intense emotions related to attraction, love, and rejection, which can contribute to their overall emotional growth.

Certainly! Here's a story that captures the intense emotions of adolescence related to attraction, love, and rejection, and how these experiences contribute to emotional growth:

3.5.4 The Heart's Echo

At sixteen, Ava felt the weight of her world shift with the arrival of a new student at her high school. His name was Liam, and with his warm smile and effortless charm, he seemed to captivate everyone around him. Ava found herself drawn to him in a way she had never experienced before. Her heart would race whenever she saw him in the hallways, and she spent countless hours daydreaming about him.

One day, after weeks of trying to muster the courage, Ava finally found herself in a conversation with Liam. To her surprise, he was friendly and genuinely interested in what she had to say. They talked about their favourite books, shared laughs, and for a fleeting moment, Ava felt a connection she had only read about in novels.

As the days passed, Ava found herself caught in a whirlwind of emotions. Her friends noticed her distracted and giddy, but Ava couldn't help it. She began to imagine a future with Liam, filled with shared moments and whispered secrets. The intensity of her feelings was both thrilling and overwhelming.

One Friday evening, Liam invited Ava to a school dance. Her excitement was palpable, and she spent hours preparing, hoping that this night would be the beginning of something special. The dance was magical, with twinkling lights and soft music filling the room. As the night progressed, Liam's attention seemed to drift. He danced with other girls, laughed with his friends, and seemed distant from Ava.

At the end of the night, Liam walked Ava to her car. He thanked her for coming and gave her a polite hug. Ava's heart sank. She had hoped for a different ending, one where they would share a special moment or perhaps a deeper connection. Instead, she felt a pang of rejection that left her feeling empty and confused.

The next few days were a blur of mixed emotions. Ava grappled with feelings of sadness and self-doubt. She wondered if she had misread the signs or if there was something wrong with her. Her friends offered comfort, but the experience left her questioning her worth and her understanding of love and attraction.

In the weeks that followed, Ava began to reflect on the experience. She realised that her feelings for Liam had been intense, but perhaps they were also idealised. She understood that attraction and love could be powerful, but they didn't always turn out the way one hopes. This experience, though painful, taught her valuable lessons about herself and about relationships.

Ava learned that rejection was not a reflection of her value, but rather a part of growing up and learning about the complexities of human emotions. She began to embrace her own strengths and to appreciate the importance of self-worth beyond external validation. Through her experience with Liam, Ava grew emotionally, developing resilience and a deeper understanding of what she truly sought in relationships.

As she moved forward, Ava approached her interactions with more confidence and clarity. She knew that the journey of adolescence was filled with highs and lows, but each experience was a stepping stone in her emotional growth. And as she navigated the intricate dance of attraction, love, and rejection, she found her heart growing stronger and wiser.

3.5.5 Aspects of Emotional Support

All aspects of emotional support are important and interconnected, contributing to a child's overall emotional well-being and development. Unconditional love and affection provide a strong emotional foundation, while open communication fosters trust and self-expression. Positive reinforcement boosts self-esteem, and empathy and understanding help children feel heard and validated. Consistency and stability reduce anxiety, and healthy relationships teach positive interaction skills. Emotional literacy and coping skills are vital for managing emotions and building resilience. Encouraging independence and autonomy fosters competence, while play and creativity support cognitive and emotional growth. Physical health impacts emotional well-being, and social skills are crucial for forming healthy relationships. Education and learning promote intellectual growth and a sense of accomplishment, and role models and mentors offer guidance and inspiration. A balanced and holistic approach to these aspects ensures comprehensive support for a child's overall well-being. While all aspects are important, the emphasis on each may shift based on the individual child's circumstances and developmental stage. The goal is to provide a balanced and holistic approach to emotional support, ensuring that the child's overall well-being is nurtured in a comprehensive manner. While all aspects of emotional support are crucial, discussing infatuation and attraction to the opposite-sex holds a unique and significant role. Infatuation, a natural part of growing up, plays a significant role in a child's emotional and social development. Addressing infatuation early on helps children understand and navigate their emotions, fostering emotional intelligence and self-awareness. By discussing infatuation, caregivers can guide children in recognising and managing their feelings in healthy ways, promoting positive relationship skills such as respect, empathy, and boundaries. This early guidance helps prevent potential emotional distress or confusion as children encounter these feelings, equipping them with the tools to form healthy, respectful relationships in the future. Integrating discussions about infatuation into the broader context of emotional support ensures that children are better prepared to handle complex emotions, contributing to their overall emotional well-being and resilience.

3.5.6 Complex and Weak Emotions

Infatuation and attraction to the opposite-sex are pivotal in a child's transition from childhood to adolescence, marking a critical phase of emotional and social development. Unlike the more constant aspects of emotional support such as unconditional love, stability, and physical health, infatuation and attraction are dynamic and can profoundly impact a child's self-esteem and relationships. Addressing these feelings helps children understand and manage complex emotions, fostering emotional intelligence, which is essential for navigating social interactions and building healthy relationships. Open discussions about infatuation and attraction are instrumental in teaching children about boundaries, consent, and respect, which are foundational for any healthy relationship. Moreover, this aspect of emotional support prepares children to deal with potential emotional challenges, reducing anxiety and confusion associated with these new experiences. While all areas of emotional support contribute to a child's well-being, understanding and managing infatuation and attraction specifically equip children with critical life skills for their present and future relationships, making it an indispensable component of their emotional growth.

3.5.7 How can I Start this Conversation?

Starting a conversation about infatuation and attraction to the opposite-sex with a girl child can be approached with sensitivity, openness, and age-appropriate language. Here are some steps to help initiate this discussion:

1. **Create a Comfortable Environment**: Choose a relaxed and private setting where the child feels safe and at ease. This could be during a casual walk, at home in a comfortable space, or any environment where distractions are minimal.

2. **Use Open-Ended Questions**: Begin with general questions about friendships and feelings to gauge the child's current understanding and comfort level. For example, "Have you noticed any changes in how you feel about your friends lately?"

3. **Share Personal Experiences**: Sharing your own experiences or stories can make the conversation feel more relatable and less intimidating. You might say, "When I was your age, I remember feeling confused about liking someone. It's completely normal."

4. **Normalise the Feelings**: Emphasise that infatuation and attraction are natural parts of growing up. Assure the child that everyone experiences these feelings and it's okay to talk about them. For instance, "It's normal to have crushes or feel attracted to someone. Everyone goes through it."

5. **Focus on Emotions and Respect**: Discuss the importance of understanding and managing these feelings, as well as respecting oneself and others. You could say, "It's important to recognise our feelings and also understand how to respect others' feelings and boundaries."

6. **Be a Good Listener**: Encourage the child to ask questions and share their thoughts. Listen actively and validate their feelings. For example, "I'm here to listen to any questions or thoughts you have. It's important to talk about these things."

7. **Introduce Key Concepts**: Gradually introduce concepts like consent, boundaries, and healthy relationships. You might explain, "When we like someone, it's important to respect their boundaries and understand that everyone feels differently."

8. **Offer Reassurance**: Reassure the child that they can come to you with any questions or concerns in the future. Let them know that these conversations can continue as they grow and their feelings evolve.

9. **Provide Resources**: Offer age-appropriate books, articles, or other resources that can help explain these topics further. Suggest, "If you're curious, there are some great books we can read together about growing up and feelings."

10. **Follow-Up**: Keep the lines of communication open and check in regularly to see how they are feeling and if they have any new questions. You might say, "We can talk about this anytime you want. I'm always here for you."

Starting a conversation about infatuation and attraction with a young girl can be approached with warmth, sensitivity, and openness. Begin by creating a comfortable, private setting to put her at ease, then gently introduce the topic through open-ended questions about friendships and feelings to gauge her comfort level. Sharing a personal experience can make the conversation more relatable, helping her feel less alone in her emotions. Emphasise that feelings of attraction and curiosity are natural and a normal part of growing up. Focus on understanding emotions, respect, and boundaries, while actively listening to her thoughts and questions. Gradually introduce concepts like consent and healthy relationships, offering reassurance that she can always come to you for guidance. Supporting her with age-appropriate resources and following up regularly can keep communication open and help her navigate her emotions confidently.

Here's an example of how to start the conversation:

"Hey [Child's Name], I've noticed you've been spending more time with [Friend's Name] lately. Have you noticed any new feelings about your friends or anyone else? It's completely normal to start having different kinds of feelings about people as you get older. When I was your age, I felt the same way, and sometimes it was confusing. If you ever want to talk about it or have questions, I'm here for you."

Parents play a crucial role in supporting their children through the emotional ups and downs of adolescence. Here's how they can identify and help their children navigate this challenging period.

Identifying Emotional Struggles

1. **Behavioural Changes**: Look for changes in behaviour, such as withdrawal from friends and family, changes in sleep patterns, or a drop in academic performance. These can be signs of emotional distress.

2. **Mood Swings**: Notice if your child experiences frequent mood swings or seems unusually irritable, sad, or anxious. Intense emotional reactions can indicate underlying issues.

3. **Communication Patterns**: Pay attention to changes in how your child communicates. If they become less open or start avoiding conversations about their feelings, it could signal emotional struggles.

4. **Social Interactions**: Observe their interactions with peers. Issues such as difficulties in friendships, conflicts, or problems related to romantic relationships can affect emotional well-being.

5. **Physical Symptoms**: Be aware of physical symptoms that might accompany emotional issues, such as headaches, stomach aches, or changes in appetite.

Identifying emotional struggles in adolescents is essential, as this phase of life is marked by rapid changes, intense emotions, and newfound pressures. Recognising the signs of distress early can help provide the support they need to navigate these challenges healthily. One of the first indicators to watch for is **behavioural changes**. Adolescents may withdraw from their usual social activities, spending less time with family and friends. They might seem more isolated, preferring to stay alone or avoiding conversations altogether. Academic performance can also be a clue; a sudden decline in grades or a lack of interest in schoolwork might indicate that they're preoccupied with emotional concerns rather than academic goals. Sleep patterns can shift as well, with some adolescents experiencing insomnia or excessive sleep, both of which can be signs of stress, anxiety, or depression.

Mood swings are another prominent feature of adolescent development and can sometimes be challenging to distinguish from typical teenage behaviour. However, when mood swings become frequent or unusually intense—manifesting as heightened irritability, sudden sadness, or anxiety—it could be a sign of deeper emotional struggles. Adolescents often have difficulty regulating their emotions, particularly if they are dealing with stressors they haven't encountered before. If they seem overwhelmed or are having frequent emotional outbursts, they may need guidance in processing their feelings.

Communication patterns also offer valuable insights. If a child who was once open and talkative becomes reserved, it may signal that they're grappling with difficult emotions. They might avoid conversations about certain topics, especially if they sense they will not be fully understood or fear judgement. Avoiding discussions about feelings or minimising their importance can sometimes be a way to cope with emotional pain they aren't ready to face or share.

Another area to pay attention to is their **social interactions**. Adolescents often place high importance on their peer relationships, and difficulties here can have a significant impact on their emotional well-being. For example, if an adolescent faces conflicts with friends, struggles to maintain friendships, or has issues related to romantic relationships, they may feel isolated or experience self-doubt. Social challenges can be a major source of stress, especially if they feel rejected, misunderstood, or pressured to conform to certain peer expectations. These situations can create intense feelings of loneliness, anxiety, or confusion.

Physical symptoms often accompany emotional distress, even if the adolescent doesn't directly link the two. Headaches, stomachaches, and changes in appetite can be psychosomatic symptoms, meaning they are physical manifestations of emotional issues. When these symptoms occur frequently without a medical cause, they may be a sign that the adolescent is under considerable stress. For instance, an adolescent experiencing prolonged anxiety may develop tension headaches or digestive issues as their body responds to the stress.

Identifying these signs early on is crucial to providing timely and appropriate support. Adolescents benefit from open, non-judgemental communication where they feel comfortable sharing their struggles. When parents, caregivers, and teachers are mindful of these indicators, they can create an environment that promotes self-expression and emotional awareness. Recognising the signs and offering gentle support can help adolescents feel understood and guide them towards healthy coping strategies, ultimately leading them towards resilience and emotional growth.

Helping Teens Navigate Emotional Challenges

1. Open Communication

Creating an environment where a teen feels safe to share their thoughts and feelings is one of the most important steps in supporting them through emotional challenges. An open line of communication allows them to express themselves without fear of judgement or punishment. It's crucial to listen actively when they talk, making eye contact and offering empathy rather than trying to solve their problems immediately. Teens are more likely to share their emotions when they know they won't be criticised, so it's essential to validate their feelings. Let them know that their emotions are natural and that they have the right to feel however they feel. This reassurance can help them build emotional awareness and trust.

2. Provide Reassurance

Adolescents often grapple with overwhelming emotions such as anxiety, sadness, or anger. During these times, offering reassurance is critical.

Remind them that these feelings, though intense, are temporary and common among teens. You can share that many others have gone through similar emotional struggles and emerged stronger. A gentle reminder that it's okay to feel vulnerable and ask for help can alleviate the pressure teens may feel to 'have it all together'. Reassurance can also come in the form of reminding them that they are not alone in their experiences.

3. Encourage Emotional Expression

Emotional expression is key to emotional regulation and mental well-being. Encourage your teen to find healthy outlets to express their emotions. Talking is an obvious method, but not all teens are comfortable with verbal expression. Writing in a journal, creating artwork, or engaging in physical activities like dancing or sports can also help them channel their feelings constructively. Find out what works best for your child, and support their efforts in engaging with these forms of expression. This teaches them that their feelings deserve to be acknowledged, and it gives them an effective way to cope with stress.

4. Teach Coping Strategies

Coping skills are crucial for emotional well-being. As a parent or mentor, it's essential to help your teen develop tools to manage stress and difficult emotions. Techniques like deep breathing, mindfulness meditation, and progressive muscle relaxation can reduce anxiety and promote emotional stability. Problem-solving skills can help them approach challenges with a clearer mindset. Encourage your teen to practice these strategies regularly, not just in moments of distress. Over time, these techniques can become automatic responses to emotional upheavals, empowering teens to take control of their emotional well-being.

5. Set a Positive Example

Teens often mirror the behaviour of adults around them. By modelling healthy emotional management and problem-solving skills, you provide a blueprint for your child to follow. Show them how to express feelings in a calm and constructive manner. When faced with challenges, demonstrate how to approach problems thoughtfully and positively. Let your teen see how you manage your own emotions, cope with stress, and take care of your mental health. By witnessing these actions, teens learn how to regulate their emotions and develop healthy coping mechanisms for themselves.

6. Monitor Social Media Use

In today's digital age, social media can have a profound effect on a teen's emotional well-being. Constant comparisons to others, online bullying, and the pressure to project a 'perfect' image can negatively impact self-esteem. Encourage your teen to use social media mindfully, focusing on positive content and avoiding toxic environments. Set boundaries around screen time to ensure that social media doesn't become an emotional crutch or source of stress. Talk to them about the importance of taking breaks from screens and maintaining a balance between online and offline interactions. Encourage them to engage in face-to-face connections with friends and family as these relationships often provide more meaningful emotional support.

7. Encourage Healthy Relationships

The relationships that teens form with their peers are incredibly important for their emotional development. Positive friendships offer a support system during times of emotional turmoil and can help reduce feelings of loneliness or isolation. Encourage your teen to seek out friendships with peers who value kindness, mutual respect, and open communication. Help them navigate any challenges in their social circles, teaching them how to resolve conflicts healthily and set boundaries. Let them know it's okay to walk away from toxic relationships and that their emotional health comes first.

8. Seek Professional Help

While parents and guardians can provide valuable support, sometimes emotional struggles may require the expertise of a mental health professional. If your teen shows signs of persistent distress, such as a significant decline in mood, changes in behaviour, or withdrawal from activities, it may be time to seek professional help. A counsellor or therapist can help your teen explore the underlying causes of their emotional challenges and teach them coping strategies tailored to their individual needs. Therapy can provide a safe space for teens to talk openly and work through their emotions with someone who is trained to offer support.

9. Promote Healthy Habits

Physical health and emotional health are closely linked. Encourage your teen to engage in regular physical activity, as exercise releases endorphins, which help regulate mood. A balanced diet, adequate hydration, and sufficient sleep are all crucial factors in maintaining emotional well-being. Help your teen develop a routine that includes time for relaxation, self-care, and sleep. Teaching them the importance of caring for their physical health will also benefit their mental health, making it easier for them to manage emotional challenges.

10. Foster Self-Esteem

Self-esteem is a vital aspect of emotional resilience. Help your teen develop a positive self-image by acknowledging their strengths and accomplishments, no matter how small. Encourage them to pursue activities or hobbies that make them feel confident and empowered. Whether it's through sports, art, academics, or volunteer work, having a sense of purpose and achievement builds self-esteem and resilience. Teach them to embrace their uniqueness and value themselves for who they are, rather than for external approval or comparisons to others.

Conclusion

Supporting teens through emotional challenges is an ongoing process that requires patience, understanding, and guidance. By fostering open communication, teaching coping strategies, encouraging emotional expression, and promoting healthy habits, you can help your teen develop the emotional intelligence and resilience they need to navigate adolescence successfully. With the right support, they can emerge from this developmental stage not only equipped with the tools to manage their emotions but also with a stronger sense of self and a more positive outlook on life.

Chapter 4

PRACTICAL STRATEGIES FOR FOSTERING EMOTIONAL INTELLIGENCE

4.1 RECOGNISING AND NAMING EMOTIONS

- **Emotion Identification Games**: Children often struggle to recognise emotions in themselves and others, especially if they lack the vocabulary to describe them. By playing games like 'emotion charades' or using flashcards with facial expressions, children can practice identifying feelings such as happiness, sadness, anger, or surprise. Additionally, role-playing scenarios where children act out emotions can help them relate feelings to real-life experiences, making emotional recognition more intuitive.

- **Daily Emotion Check-ins**: Regularly asking children to reflect on their emotions helps build emotional awareness. During family discussions or classroom activities, a simple question like, "How are you feeling today?" allows children to identify and share their emotions. This habit encourages them to acknowledge their internal state and learn to differentiate between various emotions throughout the day. For younger children, using a visual emotion chart where they can point to the face that represents their feelings can be particularly effective.

- **Emotion Vocabulary**: Expanding a child's emotional vocabulary is essential for them to articulate what they are feeling more accurately. Teaching words beyond basic emotions (e.g., anxious, frustrated, excited, proud) gives children the tools to express subtle differences in how they feel. This practice also improves their communication skills when dealing with others, allowing them to explain their emotions in a way that leads to better understanding and support from peers and adults.

4.2 DEVELOPING EMPATHY

- **Perspective-Taking Exercises**: One of the most effective ways to develop empathy is by encouraging children to see situations from someone else's perspective. After a story or interaction, ask children questions like, "How do you think that person felt?" or "What would you do if you were in their shoes?" This helps children understand that other people may have different feelings and viewpoints, even in the same situation. It promotes emotional connection and awareness of others' experiences, fostering compassion.

- **Role-Playing**: Engaging in role-playing scenarios allows children to practice empathy in a controlled environment. For example, have a child pretend to be a friend who is feeling sad or upset, while another child or adult practices providing comfort or support. This technique teaches children how to respond appropriately to the emotions of others and strengthens their social skills, helping them navigate interpersonal relationships with greater sensitivity.

- **Service Activities**: Participating in community service projects or acts of kindness—such as helping a neighbour or participating in a charity event—can deeply influence a child's understanding of empathy. By witnessing or experiencing the challenges that others face, children can develop a sense of responsibility and emotional connection towards others. This not only strengthens their empathy but also teaches them the importance of giving back to their community and helping those in need.

4.3 MANAGING STRESS AND ANXIETY

- **Breathing and Relaxation Techniques**: Teaching children how to manage their stress and anxiety is crucial for their emotional development. Simple breathing exercises like 'belly breathing' (where they place their hand on their stomach to feel it rise and fall) or 'counting breaths' can help children calm down when they feel overwhelmed. Progressive muscle relaxation, where children tense and release different muscle groups, can also reduce tension and anxiety. These techniques help children regain control over their emotions and learn that they can regulate their responses to stress.

- **Journaling or Art Therapy**: Encouraging children to express their emotions through writing or drawing provides them with a safe outlet to process their feelings. Journaling can help older children reflect on their day and better understand how different events made them feel. For younger children, drawing can be a powerful way to express emotions that they might not yet have the words to describe. Both journaling and art can help children gain perspective on their emotions and provide a release for pent-up stress or anxiety.

- **Routine Building**: Consistent routines create a sense of stability and security for children, which can help reduce anxiety. Regular schedules for activities such as bedtime, meals, and study time provide predictability, helping children feel more in control of their environment. This is especially important for children who may become anxious when they are unsure of what to expect. Establishing routines teaches children time management and helps them develop healthy habits for self-care and emotional regulation.

4.4 CONFLICT RESOLUTION TECHNIQUES

- **'I' Statements**: When children express their emotions during conflicts, teaching them to use 'I' statements helps them communicate without accusing or blaming others. For example, instead of saying "You made me angry," they can say "I feel upset when you don't listen to me." This approach focuses on their own feelings and experiences rather than placing blame, reducing defensiveness and encouraging more constructive dialogue. 'I' statements empower children to own their emotions and express themselves calmly.

- **Active Listening**: Active listening is an essential skill for resolving conflicts. Teaching children to truly listen—by repeating back what they heard, asking clarifying questions, or summarising the other person's feelings—ensures that both sides feel heard and understood. This approach also prevents misunderstandings, as children learn to focus on what the other person is saying instead of simply waiting for their turn to speak. Active listening fosters empathy and cooperation, helping children approach conflicts with an open mind.

- **Problem-Solving Steps**: Conflict resolution is more effective when children are equipped with problem-solving skills. Teach them to break down the conflict into manageable steps: first, identify the problem, then brainstorm possible solutions, and finally, choose the best course of action together. This method encourages collaboration and creative thinking, empowering children to approach conflicts with confidence. It also reinforces the idea that conflicts can be resolved through peaceful discussion rather than emotional outbursts or avoidance.

Chapter 5

ACTIVITIES TO BUILD EMOTIONAL INTELLIGENCE

5.1 ROLE-PLAYING EXERCISES

Role-playing is a powerful way to build emotional intelligence by allowing children to step into someone else's shoes and explore different emotions and perspectives. It can be done in various settings—at home, in the classroom, or during group activities. These exercises help children practice empathy, emotional regulation, and communication.

- **Example Activity**: Create a scenario where a child might encounter an emotionally challenging situation, such as a disagreement with a friend or feeling left out in a group. Ask the child to act out how they would feel and respond in that situation. Then, switch roles and have the child play the other person involved. After the role-play, discuss what emotions were felt and how each person's response affected the situation. This helps children understand the impact of emotions on behaviour and relationships.

- **Benefit**: This activity encourages emotional awareness and helps children practice responding to others with empathy and understanding. It also enhances their ability to navigate social situations with greater emotional intelligence.

5.2 JOURNALING PROMPTS

Journaling is a reflective activity that helps children process their emotions and understand their inner thoughts. By responding to specific prompts, children can articulate their feelings, reflect on their experiences, and become more self-aware.

- **Example Activity**: Provide children with prompts such as:
  - "What made you feel proud today?"
  - "Describe a time you felt frustrated. What did you do to manage it?"
  - "What emotions did you experience this week, and how did you handle them?" Encourage them to write freely without worrying about grammar or structure. Younger children can use drawing as a form of journaling by creating pictures to express their feelings.
- **Benefit**: Journaling promotes emotional expression and introspection, helping children develop a deeper understanding of their emotions. It also provides a safe outlet for processing challenging experiences, reducing stress and enhancing emotional regulation.

5.3 MINDFULNESS PRACTICES

Mindfulness helps children focus on the present moment, which can improve their ability to manage stress and regulate their emotions.

Regular mindfulness practices teach children how to observe their thoughts and feelings without judgement, fostering self-awareness and emotional control.

- **Example Activity**: Introduce a simple mindfulness practice such as 'belly breathing', where children place their hands on their stomachs and focus on the rise and fall of their breath. You can also guide them through a 'body scan', where they pay attention to different parts of their body, noticing how they feel. Another fun mindfulness exercise is 'mindful eating', where children focus on the taste, texture, and smell of their food to stay in the present moment.

- **Benefit**: Mindfulness practices help children calm their minds and bodies, reducing anxiety and enhancing their ability to focus. It also teaches them to pause and reflect before reacting emotionally, leading to better emotional regulation.

5.4 EMOTION RECOGNITION GAMES

Games that focus on recognising emotions help children develop the ability to identify and understand different feelings in themselves and others. These games make learning about emotions fun and interactive, helping children build emotional literacy in a playful environment.

- **Example Activity**: Play a game where children are shown pictures of people expressing different emotions (happy, sad, angry, surprised, etc.) and asked to name the emotion. You can also act out various emotions and have children guess which emotion is being portrayed. Another option is the 'Emotion Charades' game, where one child acts out an emotion without speaking, and others guess what it is.

- **Benefit**: These games improve children's ability to recognise emotions from facial expressions, body language, and tone of voice. Developing this skill is essential for building empathy, improving communication, and strengthening relationships.

Chapter 6

PARENTING TECHNIQUES FOR EMOTIONAL GROWTH

6.1 EFFECTIVE COMMUNICATION STRATEGIES

Communication is at the heart of fostering emotional growth in children. By practising effective communication, parents can help children feel heard, understood, and supported, which is crucial for emotional development.

- **Example Technique**: Use open-ended questions when talking with your child to encourage deeper conversations. Instead of asking yes/no questions like, "Did you have a good day?" ask, "What was the best part of your day?" or "How did that make you feel?" These types of questions promote emotional reflection and open the door to meaningful discussions.

- **Benefit**: This approach helps children learn to articulate their feelings and thoughts clearly. It also strengthens the parent-child bond by demonstrating that their emotions are valued and important.

Effective communication involves not just talking, but engaging in meaningful, two-way exchanges that promote emotional reflection.

It helps children feel understood and teaches them how to express their own thoughts and emotions clearly.

- **Practical Applications:**

1. **During Daily Conversations**: At dinner or bedtime, ask your child open-ended questions that prompt reflection on their day. For example, "What made you smile today?" or "Was there anything that made you feel upset? Why?" This approach invites them to share deeper emotions rather than simple facts.

2. **When Addressing Misbehaviour**: Instead of immediately disciplining, asks your child, "What were you feeling when that happened?" and "What could you do next time?" This encourages problem-solving and emotional awareness.

3. **In Emotional Situations**: When your child is upset or crying, instead of saying "Stop crying," try "Can you tell me what's making you sad?" This allows them to express themselves and fosters emotional openness.

- **Key Tip**: Always avoid dismissing or minimising their feelings. Instead of saying, "It's no big deal," try validating their emotions with, "I understand why you feel that way."

Impact:

By practising these strategies, you help your child learn to communicate emotions and thoughts in a healthy way, which enhances emotional intelligence and strengthens the parent-child relationship.

Fostering emotional growth in children starts with effective communication. When children feel genuinely heard and understood, they develop greater emotional intelligence, resilience, and self-awareness. Effective communication goes beyond simple exchanges—it's about building a safe environment where children feel valued, where their emotions are validated, and where they can learn to express themselves openly. Here's a guide to enhancing emotional growth through intentional, meaningful communication with children.

Importance of Open-Ended Questions

One of the most powerful tools in communication is using open-ended questions. These questions encourage children to reflect, explore their feelings, and communicate more than just surface-level responses. For example, instead of asking a yes-or-no question like, "Did you have a good day?" consider asking, "What was the best part of your day?" or "How did that experience make you feel?" This type of questioning invites children to think deeper and share more about their experiences, emotions, and thoughts.

Benefit: Open-ended questions help children articulate their feelings, which is key for developing emotional literacy. This approach not only provides insight into their inner world but also reinforces the idea that their emotions matter. When children feel that their perspectives and emotions are valued, it strengthens the bond with their parents, creating a supportive environment for emotional growth.

Practical Applications for Effective Communication

1. In Daily Conversations

Using open-ended questions during daily routines, like dinner or bedtime, provides a consistent opportunity for meaningful connection. Asking questions such as "What made you smile today?" or "Was there anything that upset you?" invites your child to discuss not only the events of their day but also the emotions associated with those events. This practice allows children to build self-reflection skills and express emotions naturally within everyday conversations.

2. When Addressing Misbehaviour

In moments of misbehaviour, instead of immediately reacting with discipline, ask questions that encourage your child to reflect on the emotions and motivations behind their actions. For instance, try asking, "What were you feeling when that happened?" or "What could you do differently next time?" This approach helps children connect their actions with their emotions, promoting emotional awareness and teaching problem-solving skills. Rather than merely correcting behaviour, you're helping them understand the emotional drivers behind their choices and providing them with tools for self-regulation.

3. In Emotional Situations

When a child is visibly upset or crying, it's natural to want to comfort them quickly, but dismissive language like "Stop crying" can make them feel that their emotions are unwelcome. Instead, try saying, "Can you tell me what's making you feel sad?" or "I'm here to listen whenever you're ready." This approach encourages them to share their feelings openly and reassures them that their emotions are valid. It also cultivates emotional openness, showing them that expressing sadness, frustration, or anger is safe and acceptable.

Key Tips for Effective Emotional Communication

1. **Avoid Minimising Feelings:** Phrases like "It's no big deal" or "You're overreacting" can make children feel that their emotions are unimportant. Instead, validate their feelings by saying things like, "I can see why you feel that way" or "I understand that this is hard for you." Validating emotions teaches children to respect their own feelings, an essential aspect of emotional intelligence.

2. **Practice Active Listening:** Show your child that you are fully present and engaged by maintaining eye contact, nodding, and

responding thoughtfully. When children sense that you are genuinely listening, they feel respected and more inclined to share openly.

3. **Create a Judgement-Free Zone:** Avoid being overly critical or giving immediate advice when your child shares their feelings. Sometimes they may just need a safe space to vent and explore their thoughts without receiving solutions. Ask if they would like help with a solution or if they just want you to listen.

Impact of Effective Communication on Emotional Growth

By practising these strategies, you create a foundation for emotional resilience and intelligence in your child. Effective communication encourages children to become aware of and articulate their emotions, a skill that is crucial for handling complex feelings and interpersonal relationships as they grow. When children learn to express their thoughts and emotions clearly, they also develop empathy and a better understanding of others' emotions, strengthening social connections and building emotional maturity.

Moreover, these communication techniques strengthen the parent-child relationship. Children who feel understood are more likely to trust and confide in their parents as they navigate life's challenges. This trust not only supports them during childhood but also fosters a lasting bond as they transition into adolescence and adulthood. By guiding children to communicate their emotions healthily and openly, parents lay the groundwork for lifelong emotional wellness and resilience.

6.2 ACTIVE LISTENING SKILLS

Active listening involves giving full attention to your child when they speak, making them feel acknowledged and respected. This builds trust and encourages open emotional expression.

- **Example Technique**: When your child is sharing something, stop what you're doing, maintain eye contact, and listen without interrupting. After they've finished speaking, reflect back what you've heard by saying, "It sounds like you're feeling frustrated because..." or "I can see that this made you really happy." This confirms to the child that you understand their feelings and are fully present in the conversation.

- **Benefit**: Active listening helps children feel validated, promoting emotional security. It also teaches them how to listen empathetically to others, which is a critical part of emotional intelligence.

Active listening is crucial for building trust and showing children that their feelings matter. It's more than just hearing what they say; it's engaging with their words, understanding their emotions, and responding thoughtfully.

- **Practical Applications:**

1. **When Your Child Needs to Vent**: If your child comes to you frustrated about a situation at school, instead of immediately offering advice, listen without interruption. After they finish, reflect back by saying, "I can see that you're feeling really frustrated because your friend didn't include you." This shows empathy and encourages them to keep sharing.

2. **During Conflicts**: If your child argues with a sibling or friend, actively listen to both sides before offering a solution. Ask, "Can you tell me how you're feeling about what happened?" This helps them feel heard and teaches them to listen to others as well.

3. **In Problem-Solving Situations**: When your child expresses frustration with a task (like homework), listen patiently and ask

clarifying questions like, "What's making this hard for you?" instead of immediately solving the problem for them.

- **Key Tip**: Avoid multitasking when listening to your child. Giving them your full attention communicates that their emotions and thoughts are important.

Impact:

Active listening validates your child's feelings, which helps them feel more secure and promotes their ability to empathise and listen actively in their own interactions.

Active listening is a powerful communication skill that strengthens the parent-child bond and fosters a secure emotional environment. By giving your child undivided attention and genuinely engaging with what they say, you communicate that their feelings and experiences matter. Active listening is more than simply hearing their words; it involves understanding their emotions, responding empathetically, and demonstrating respect for their perspective. When children feel fully listened to, they are more likely to open up and trust that they can share both positive and challenging emotions without fear of dismissal.

One effective approach to active listening is to stop what you're doing when your child speaks, make eye contact, and listen without interrupting. Once they finish, you can reflect their feelings back by saying something like, "It sounds like you're feeling frustrated because…" or "I can see this made you really happy." This reflective response not only validates their emotions but also shows that you're fully present in the conversation. By practising this technique, you let your child know that their thoughts are valued and understood, which promotes a sense of emotional security.

Active listening can be applied in various everyday situations, from moments when your child simply needs to vent, to conflicts with peers, or during problem-solving challenges. When your child approaches you frustrated about a situation, like a misunderstanding with a friend, resist the urge to jump in with advice or solutions. Instead, let them talk without interruption and then acknowledge their feelings with empathy. For instance, you might say, "I understand that you're feeling left out because your friend didn't include you." This empathetic response helps your child feel seen and validated, encouraging them to keep sharing openly.

During conflicts, whether with siblings or friends, active listening is an excellent tool to help resolve tensions. By giving each child the chance to express their side of the story and listening to them equally, you teach them that their feelings are valid while also modelling how to listen empathetically to others. After they share, you might say, "I understand why you felt upset when that happened." This not only eases immediate tension but also helps them develop skills to manage and communicate their feelings constructively.

In situations where your child is facing a problem, such as struggling with homework, listening actively without immediately offering a solution can be equally beneficial. Instead of solving the issue for them, ask clarifying questions like, "What's making this hard for you?" This encourages them to identify the specific issue and fosters problem-solving skills, building their confidence and independence.

A key aspect of active listening is to avoid multitasking during these interactions. When you stop other activities and give your full attention, it communicates to your child that their thoughts are a priority. This simple gesture strengthens trust and reinforces that their emotions are important.

The impact of active listening goes beyond the immediate conversation. By consistently practising these skills, you are helping your child feel emotionally secure, teaching them that their feelings are valid, and modelling how to listen and respond empathetically. This builds their emotional intelligence, making them more likely to empathise with others and develop healthy communication habits of their own. Active listening not only validates your child's feelings but also nurtures their ability to form secure relationships and strengthens the foundation for positive, open parent-child communication as they grow.

6.3 MODELLING EMOTIONAL INTELLIGENCE

Children learn emotional behaviours by observing their parents. Modelling emotional intelligence—such as expressing feelings appropriately, managing stress, and showing empathy—teaches children how to handle their own emotions effectively.

- **Example Technique**: When you experience emotions, narrate them to your child in a constructive way. For example, if you're feeling frustrated, say, "I'm feeling a bit frustrated right now because things aren't going as planned, but I'm going to take a deep breath and figure it out." This shows the child that it's okay to feel emotions and demonstrates how to manage them in a healthy way.

- **Benefit**: Children who see their parents handle emotions with patience, empathy, and thoughtfulness are more likely to develop similar emotional coping strategies. Modelling emotional intelligence teaches by example, reinforcing the skills children need for their own emotional growth.

Children learn by example, so modelling emotional intelligence is one of the most powerful ways to teach it. Parents can demonstrate how to manage emotions, respond empathetically, and communicate feelings healthily.

- **Practical Applications:**

1. **Handling Stress or Anger**: If you're feeling stressed, say out loud, "I'm feeling a little stressed right now, so I'm going to take a few deep breaths to calm down." This models self-regulation techniques for managing emotions, showing your child that it's okay to feel overwhelmed but important to handle it constructively.

2. **Demonstrating Empathy**: When someone in the family is upset, talk about how that person might be feeling. For instance, "Your brother is feeling sad because he lost his toy. How do you think we can help him feel better?" This encourages empathy by illustrating compassionate behaviour.

3. **Expressing Your Own Emotions**: Let your child see that you express emotions in healthy ways. For example, "I felt really happy when I saw you helping your sister today. It made me proud." This models positive reinforcement and the importance of sharing emotions.

- **Key Tip**: Be transparent with your emotions, but ensure that you model calmness and problem-solving. It's okay for children to see you experience emotions, as long as they also see you managing them.

Impact:

By modelling emotional intelligence, you teach your child how to manage their own emotions, express feelings in a constructive way, and develop empathy for others. This creates an emotionally stable environment that fosters emotional growth.

Modelling emotional intelligence is one of the most impactful ways parents can nurture emotional growth in their children. Since children learn behaviours primarily by observing, parents who demonstrate effective emotional management provide a powerful example for their kids. This form of teaching goes beyond words; it shows children how to approach their own emotions, communicate feelings constructively, and respond empathetically to others. By practising emotional intelligence openly, parents create a family environment where emotions are acknowledged, valued, and managed in a healthy way.

One effective approach is to verbalise your own emotions in a constructive manner. For instance, when you experience frustration, you might say, "I'm feeling a bit frustrated right now because things aren't going as planned, but I'm going to take a deep breath and figure it out." This teaches children that it's normal to feel frustrated or disappointed and demonstrates a calm way to handle those feelings. Children who see this behaviour learn that emotions are a part of life and that managing them positively is essential. Additionally, expressing emotions aloud helps demystify feelings for children and reduces the tendency to bottle them up.

Modelling empathy is another crucial aspect of emotional intelligence. By demonstrating compassion and understanding towards others, parents show children how to connect with and support those around them. For example, if a sibling is upset, a parent might say, "Your brother is feeling sad because he lost his favourite toy. What do you think we could do to help him feel better?" This type of interaction not only encourages empathy but also engages the child in problem-solving to support someone else. It teaches children to consider how others feel and to think about ways to respond kindly, strengthening their social and emotional skills.

Expressing positive emotions and sharing them with children is equally important. When parents let their children know how their actions make them feel, it reinforces positive behaviour and the concept of emotional sharing. For example, saying, "I felt really happy and proud when I saw you helping your sister today," conveys approval and appreciation, encouraging children to repeat such positive actions. This type of reinforcement builds their self-esteem, as they learn that their actions can positively affect others, deepening their understanding of relational dynamics.

A key principle in modelling emotional intelligence is being transparent about emotions but also demonstrating control and healthy coping strategies. For instance, showing vulnerability by expressing sadness or disappointment in a calm way can teach children that all emotions are valid. At the same time, showing them that you can work through challenging emotions constructively provides a valuable lesson in resilience. For instance, if you're overwhelmed, you might explain, "I'm feeling a bit stressed, so I'm going to take a few deep breaths or go for a short walk to clear my mind." This shows children a real-life example of managing emotions rather than suppressing or ignoring them, which is crucial for developing their own emotional regulation skills.

The impact of modelling emotional intelligence is far-reaching. Children who observe their parents handling emotions with empathy, patience, and thoughtfulness are more likely to adopt these skills themselves. They learn how to manage stress, express their feelings constructively, and develop empathy for others. These skills lay the foundation for emotional stability and social resilience, equipping them with tools to navigate relationships, handle conflicts, and engage meaningfully with others as they grow. By modelling emotional intelligence, parents help create a secure and supportive environment where children feel safe to express their emotions and, in turn, are encouraged to grow into empathetic, emotionally intelligent individuals.

6.4 CREATING AN EMOTIONALLY SUPPORTIVE ENVIRONMENT

An emotionally supportive environment is one where children feel safe to express their feelings without fear of judgement or punishment. This type of environment fosters trust, emotional openness, and security, helping children develop emotional resilience.

- **Example Technique**: Establish 'emotion-safe zones' at home where children can freely talk about their feelings. Let them know that it's okay to feel sad, angry, or disappointed, and that you are there to help them work through these emotions. Validate their feelings by saying, "It's okay to feel upset; let's talk about why," rather than dismissing their emotions with phrases like "Don't cry" or "You'll be fine."

- **Benefit**: Creating a supportive emotional environment helps children develop emotional literacy and self-awareness. It also strengthens their confidence in expressing emotions, knowing they won't be judged or shamed for how they feel.

Children thrive in environments where they feel emotionally safe and supported. Creating a space where feelings are acknowledged and validated helps build emotional resilience and trust.

- **Practical Applications:**

1. **Emotion-Safe Zones**: Designate a place in your home where your child can go when they need to calm down or process emotions. Equip the space with tools like a feelings chart, calming sensory items (soft toys, stress balls), or drawing materials. When your child is overwhelmed, they can retreat to this zone to express themselves freely.

2. **Emotion-Centred Family Meetings**: Hold regular family meetings where everyone has the chance to talk about their feelings—what's going well, what challenges they're facing, and how they're handling emotions. This normalises emotional expression and encourages children to share their inner world with the family.

3. **Validating Emotions**: Whenever your child expresses an emotion, whether positive or negative, validate it. If they're angry, instead of saying "You shouldn't feel angry," try, "I see you're angry, and that's okay. Let's talk about why." This makes them feel understood and supported.

- **Key Tip**: Avoid punishing children for expressing negative emotions (e.g., anger, sadness). Instead, guide them on how to manage these emotions in a healthy way. For example, if they yell out of frustration, you can say, "I understand you're frustrated, but let's try to talk about it calmly."

Impact:

An emotionally supportive environment allows children to feel safe in expressing their emotions. This sense of security is essential for building emotional resilience, which helps them navigate emotional challenges throughout life.

Each of these techniques—effective communication, active listening, modelling emotional intelligence, and creating an emotionally supportive environment—forms a critical part of fostering emotional growth in children. When practised consistently, they not only help children build emotional intelligence but also strengthen the parent-child relationship, creating a strong foundation for lifelong emotional well-being.

Creating an emotionally supportive environment at home is essential for fostering children's emotional growth and resilience. When children feel safe expressing their emotions without fear of judgement or punishment, they are more likely to develop emotional openness, trust, and security. A supportive home environment teaches children that emotions are natural and valid, allowing them to build confidence in sharing their feelings.

One effective technique for this is establishing 'emotion-safe zones' at home where children can retreat to calm down or process emotions freely. Equipping this space with items like a feelings chart, stress-relief toys, or drawing supplies allows children to express themselves safely when they feel overwhelmed. Family meetings focused on emotional sharing are also valuable, as they provide everyone with a dedicated time to discuss what they're experiencing, making emotional expression a normalised and valued family practice. These meetings can cover highlights, challenges, and how each family member is managing their emotions, creating an open line of communication and support.

Validating children's emotions is another key element in a supportive environment. Acknowledging emotions, rather than dismissing or minimising them, reassures children that their feelings are important. For example, if a child expresses anger, responding with, "I see you're angry, and that's okay. Let's talk about why," instead of "You shouldn't feel that way," helps them feel understood and safe. This approach teaches children emotional literacy and fosters a habit of expressing and discussing their emotions constructively.

It is also essential to avoid punishing children for showing negative emotions like anger or sadness. Instead, parents can guide them toward healthier ways to handle these feelings. For instance, if a child yells out of frustration, a response like, "I understand you're frustrated, but let's talk about it calmly," can teach them that while their feelings are valid, there are more constructive ways to express them. This approach builds emotional resilience, as children learn to navigate their emotions in a balanced way without feeling ashamed.

The combined practices of effective communication, active listening, modelling emotional intelligence, and creating a supportive emotional environment form the foundation of a nurturing home. These practices allow children to grow up feeling emotionally secure, knowing that they can share their feelings openly. As a result, they develop essential emotional intelligence skills—such as empathy, self-awareness, and emotional regulation—that will help them throughout life. Furthermore, consistent application of these techniques strengthens the parent-child relationship, creating a strong, trust-based foundation that supports children's overall emotional well-being.

Chapter 7

OVERCOMING EMOTIONAL CHALLENGES

7.1 DEALING WITH PEER PRESSURE

Peer pressure can significantly impact children's emotional well-being, leading them to make choices that conflict with their values or beliefs. Teaching children how to handle peer pressure effectively is crucial for their emotional development and self-identity.

- **Practical Techniques:**

1. **Open Discussions About Values**: Regularly engage in conversations about values and principles. Ask your child, "What do you think is important when making friends?" or "How do you feel about certain behaviours?" This encourages them to think critically about their beliefs and reinforces their confidence in standing up to peer pressure.

2. **Role-Playing Scenarios**: Create hypothetical situations where your child might face peer pressure, such as being urged to try a risky behaviour. Role-play different responses with them, helping them practice saying "no" assertively and exploring alternatives, such as walking away or suggesting a different activity.

3. **Encouraging Assertiveness**: Teach your child how to assert themselves respectfully. Phrases like, "I don't feel comfortable with that" or "That's not my thing" empower them to express their feelings without fear of rejection.

- **Key Tip**: Remind your child that it's okay to stand out and make choices that are right for them, even if those choices differ from their peers. Share examples from your own life to illustrate that standing firm can lead to stronger, more genuine friendships.

7.2 BUILDING SELF-ESTEEM

A healthy self-esteem is foundational for emotional resilience. When children believe in their own worth, they are better equipped to handle challenges and setbacks.

- **Practical Techniques:**

1. **Praise Effort Over Outcome**: Focus on praising your child for their effort and perseverance rather than just the final result. For example, saying "I'm proud of how hard you worked on that project" fosters a growth mindset and reinforces their self-worth.

2. **Encourage Skills and Hobbies**: Help your child discover and pursue activities they enjoy, whether it's sports, arts, or academics. Mastering skills boosts confidence and provides a sense of accomplishment.

3. **Set Achievable Goals**: Assist your child in setting small, achievable goals. Celebrate their successes, no matter how minor, to reinforce a sense of competence and capability.

- **Key Tip**: Create an environment where mistakes are viewed as learning opportunities. Teach your child that everyone makes mistakes and that they can grow from those experiences, fostering resilience and self-acceptance.

7.3 NAVIGATING SOCIETAL EXPECTATIONS

Societal expectations can exert pressure on children, influencing their self-image and emotional health. Teaching children how to navigate these expectations is essential for fostering resilience and self-identity.

- **Practical Techniques:**

1. **Discuss Media Influence**: Talk about how media and advertising often portray unrealistic standards. Encourage your child to critically analyse what they see and understand that everyone has unique qualities that make them special.

2. **Promote Individuality**: Reinforce the idea that it's okay to be different. Share stories of people who have succeeded by being true to themselves rather than conforming to societal norms. This helps children appreciate their uniqueness and build confidence in their identity.

3. **Cultivate Critical Thinking**: Encourage your child to question societal norms. Ask them, "Why do you think people feel this way about success?" or "What do you think about this trend?" This develops their ability to think independently and reinforces their self-esteem.

- **Key Tip**: Share your own experiences of navigating societal expectations and how you overcame challenges. This can help children feel less isolated and provide them with real-life examples of resilience.

7.4 ADDRESSING BULLYING AND SOCIAL EXCLUSION

Bullying and social exclusion can have profound emotional effects on children. It's crucial to equip them with the tools and support needed to address these challenges effectively.

- **Practical Techniques:**

1. **Establish Open Communication**: Create a safe space for your child to talk about their experiences with bullying or social exclusion. Let them know that they can share without judgement and that their feelings are valid.

2. **Teach Coping Strategies**: Equip your child with coping mechanisms such as deep breathing, positive affirmations, or seeking support from trusted friends or adults when faced with bullying. Role-playing responses can also help them prepare for real-life situations.

3. **Encourage Allyship**: Teach your child the importance of standing up for themselves and others. Discuss ways they can be supportive allies to peers who may be bullied or excluded, fostering a sense of community and compassion.

- **Key Tip**: Work with the school if bullying occurs. Encourage your child to speak with a teacher or counsellor about their experiences and reinforce the idea that seeking help is a strength, not a weakness.

Helping children navigate emotional challenges such as peer pressure, self-esteem issues, societal expectations, and bullying is essential for their development into resilient, confident, and emotionally healthy individuals. One of the foundational skills in handling peer pressure is having a solid sense of personal values. Engaging children in regular discussions about what they believe and why, such as exploring questions like, "What do you think is important when making friends?" can reinforce their confidence to stand up to peer influence. Role-playing common scenarios they might encounter helps them practice assertive responses, and phrases like, "I don't feel comfortable with that," empower them to express their true feelings without fear of judgement. Teaching assertiveness and the value of staying true to oneself, even when it's challenging, strengthens their resolve to make positive choices.

Building self-esteem is another pillar of emotional well-being. By focusing praise on a child's effort rather than the outcome, you encourage a growth mindset and instil a sense of self-worth that is independent of results. This also teaches them to value hard work and resilience over perfection. Engaging in activities that they enjoy—such as sports, the arts, or academics—allows children to develop skills that build confidence through achievement. Setting small, manageable goals that are celebrated upon completion boosts self-assurance and reinforces their belief in their capabilities. An environment where mistakes are treated as learning opportunities further nurtures resilience and self-acceptance, helping children view setbacks as part of growth rather than as failures.

Societal expectations often pressure children, impacting their self-image and emotional health. By openly discussing media portrayals of 'ideal' appearances or success, children learn to question these unrealistic standards. This critical approach to media encourages them to appreciate their unique qualities, reinforcing a sense of individuality and reducing the urge to conform. Sharing stories of people who've succeeded by being themselves can inspire children to value their own differences. Fostering critical thinking through questions like, "What do you think about this trend?" helps them form independent beliefs rather than blindly following societal norms. Relating your own experiences in handling societal pressures can further empower children, making them feel understood and showing them that overcoming these challenges is possible.

Bullying and social exclusion pose significant emotional challenges, often leading to feelings of isolation and distress. Creating a home environment where children feel safe discussing bullying or social exclusion experiences is essential. Open communication assures them that their feelings are valid and provides a sense of support. Teaching them specific coping strategies, such as deep breathing and positive affirmations, helps them manage emotional responses to bullying. Role-playing assertive yet non-confrontational responses can equip them for real-life situations, empowering them to stand up for themselves effectively. Encouraging allyship, where they learn the importance of supporting peers who may be experiencing bullying, nurtures compassion and a sense of community. Working with teachers and counsellors ensures that children understand seeking help as a sign of strength, not weakness.

Each of these strategies—handling peer pressure, building self-esteem, navigating societal expectations, and addressing bullying—provides essential tools that children need to thrive emotionally. These techniques create a supportive environment, fostering resilience, self-confidence, and the ability to manage emotions. By instilling these skills early, parents lay a foundation for their children to face life's challenges with confidence and emotional strength, enhancing their overall well-being and helping them develop a balanced, positive approach to life.

Chapter 8

CASE STUDIES AND REAL-LIFE EXAMPLES

8.1 STORIES OF EMOTIONAL GROWTH

Example: *The Journey of Sarah* Once upon a time, in a small town, lived a bright and talented girl named Sarah. At 15, Sarah was like a delicate flower, yearning for sunlight but often overshadowed by dark clouds of anxiety. The weight of expectations—academic excellence and social acceptance—felt like an unbearable burden. She often found herself frozen, unable to speak up in class or join her friends at school events.

One evening, Sarah's mother noticed her withdrawn demeanour and approached her gently. "Sarah, what's on your mind?" she asked, her voice filled with concern. It was a question that opened the floodgates; Sarah poured her heart out, expressing fears of never being good enough. Instead of dismissing her feelings, her mother wrapped her in a warm embrace and encouraged her to explore her emotions through journaling.

Through the pages of her journal, Sarah began to confront her fears. Each word was a step toward healing, and soon, her parents introduced her to a compassionate counsellor. With each session, Sarah learned to recognise her feelings, breathe through the anxiety, and embrace her uniqueness.

As weeks passed, a transformation began. Sarah discovered mindfulness techniques that became her armour against the storms of self-doubt. One sunny afternoon, she decided to join the school's debate team, a step that once seemed daunting. With a quivering voice but a heart full of determination, Sarah spoke her truth in front of her peers. That day, she didn't just conquer a fear; she soared.

Sarah's journey is a testament to the power of love, understanding, and resilience. With the right support, she blossomed into a confident young woman, inspiring others to embrace their own journeys of emotional growth.

8.2 PRACTICAL APPLICATIONS OF EMOTIONAL INTELLIGENCE

Example: *The Classroom of Mr. Thompson.* In a bustling middle school filled with the sounds of laughter and the rustle of backpacks, there was a science teacher named Mr. Thompson. He had a special gift—not only for teaching science but for nurturing the emotional landscapes of his students. He understood that behind each smiling face, there were hidden struggles, dreams, and fears.

One day, he introduced a unique idea: weekly 'emotion check-ins'. Students would gather in a circle, sharing how they felt, their triumphs, and their challenges. It was a sacred space, one that allowed vulnerability to blossom. Mr. Thompson watched as the classroom transformed into a sanctuary of support and understanding.

During one of these check-ins, two students, Anna and Jake, found themselves at odds over a group project. Tension filled the air as they exchanged frustrated glances. But instead of letting anger simmer, Mr. Thompson gently intervened, reminding them of the skills they had practised in class. With newfound courage, Anna and Jake took a moment to articulate their feelings and listen to each other. They realised their shared passion for the project was greater than their disagreements.

In that moment, Mr. Thompson witnessed the magic of emotional intelligence in action. His students learned that it was okay to disagree, as long as they did so with respect and empathy. As they left the classroom that day, they carried not just knowledge of science but also valuable life lessons—tools they would use to navigate the complexities of human relationships.

8.3 LESSONS LEARNED FROM REAL-LIFE SCENARIOS

Example: *The Impact of Bullying* In a quiet neighbourhood, a bright boy named Lucas faced the harsh reality of bullying at school. Each day felt like a battle as he endured taunts and isolation from his peers. With each hurtful word, Lucas felt a piece of himself shatter, leaving him lonely and confused.

One evening, after a particularly difficult day, he came home with tears streaming down his face. His parents, sensing his pain, wrapped him in a warm embrace and encouraged him to share his feelings. It was then that Lucas found solace in art—a way to express the emotions he couldn't articulate. As he painted, he transformed his hurt into colours and shapes, each stroke telling a story of resilience and hope.

With his parents' unwavering support, Lucas decided to share his artwork in a school exhibit. When the day arrived, he stood nervously beside his creations, his heart racing. But as his classmates began to admire and discuss the pieces, something remarkable happened. Conversations about empathy and kindness blossomed, sparking discussions that reached beyond the walls of the exhibit.

Lucas's artwork became a powerful catalyst for change. Through his vulnerability, he not only found healing but also inspired others to recognise the importance of kindness. His story illustrates how expressing pain can lead to understanding and empathy, creating ripples of positivity within a community.

8.4 BUILDING EMOTIONAL RESILIENCE THROUGH REAL-LIFE EXPERIENCES

Example: *The Resilience of Emily*

Emily, a spirited 16-year-old, was used to life's ebbs and flows, but nothing could have prepared her for the storm that hit her family when financial difficulties arose. The once vibrant laughter in their home was replaced with worry and stress. Emily felt the weight of the world on her shoulders, anxiety gnawing at her spirit.

Amid the turmoil, Emily chose to find light in the darkness. She began volunteering at a local food bank, where she met families grappling with their own struggles. In that bustling kitchen, she discovered the strength of community and the power of compassion. Each interaction, each story she heard, helped her shift her perspective and reminded her that she was not alone.

As she served meals and connected with others, Emily felt her heart heal. The experience gave her a renewed sense of purpose and resilience. The anxiety that once held her captive began to fade as she learned to appreciate the beauty of human connection.

In time, Emily not only emerged stronger but also inspired her peers to join her in volunteering. Together, they organised food drives and raised awareness about the importance of kindness and support. Emily's journey from despair to empowerment exemplifies how embracing community can cultivate resilience and transform pain into purpose.

These stories illustrate the profound journey of emotional growth, showcasing how individuals navigate challenges and emerge stronger. Whether it's through the support of family, the guidance of compassionate teachers, or the power of community, these narratives remind us of the resilience of the human spirit. Each tale is a testament to the beauty of connection and the strength found in vulnerability.

Chapter 9

TOXIC RELATIONSHIPS

9.1 UNDERSTANDING TOXIC RELATIONSHIPS

A toxic relationship is any relationship that consistently harms emotional well-being. Such relationships involve patterns of manipulation, disrespect, or control, affecting one or both individuals. They can exist between friends, family members, romantic partners, or colleagues. Toxic dynamics often start subtly, making them hard to identify at first.

Example: Sarah has been in a relationship with Tom for two years. Tom is often critical of Sarah, belittling her opinions and controlling her social interactions. At first, Sarah dismisses his comments as 'tough love'. However, over time, she feels increasingly insecure and isolated, losing confidence and avoiding friends. This is a classic example of a toxic relationship where someone's self-worth is eroded over time through control and criticism.

Case Study: Raj works at a company where his boss, Alex, constantly finds faults in his work, often in front of others. Alex takes credit for Raj's successes but blames him publicly for any issues. Raj feels anxious every day at work and starts to dread his job. This toxic work relationship undermines Raj's self-esteem, showing how toxic dynamics can impact professional life.

9.2 RECOGNISING THE SIGNS OF A TOXIC RELATIONSHIP

Signs of a toxic relationship can be emotional, behavioural, or physical. Common red flags include constant criticism, controlling behaviour, manipulation, or feeling emotionally drained around a person.

Example: Jessica's best friend, Lily, often guilt-trips her for spending time with others, suggesting that Jessica 'doesn't care enough' if she can't always be there. Jessica feels anxious about upsetting Lily and over time limits her social interactions. Here, guilt-tripping is a sign of a toxic friendship where one person manipulates another by inducing guilt and emotional dependency.

Case Study: David has a romantic partner, Anna, who belittles him regularly and threatens to leave if he doesn't follow her preferences. David feels he has to walk on eggshells around her and starts losing confidence in himself. Eventually, he realises these are signs of an unhealthy relationship and seeks support to cope with the emotional damage. This case highlights how toxic relationships erode self-worth and security.

9.3 THE IMPACT OF TOXIC RELATIONSHIPS ON SELF-WORTH AND CONFIDENCE

A toxic relationship often impacts how people see themselves. Negative reinforcement, criticism, and blame can make individuals feel insecure and question their own value, leading to low self-esteem and self-doubt.

Example: Mike's partner, Nina, constantly dismisses his achievements, saying they aren't significant or valuable. Over time, Mike internalises this criticism, believing he isn't capable of success. He stops pursuing promotions at work and becomes withdrawn, fearing judgement. This example illustrates how prolonged exposure to negativity affects self-worth and motivation.

Case Study: Claire, a young professional, has a friend who always points out her flaws and makes 'jokes' about her appearance. Claire starts to feel unattractive and inadequate, leading her to avoid social events. This shows how toxic relationships can have lasting effects on confidence and self-esteem, even outside the immediate relationship.

9.4 EMOTIONAL MANIPULATION TECHNIQUES AND THEIR EFFECTS

Emotional manipulation involves using psychological tactics to control someone. Common techniques include gaslighting (making someone doubt their own reality), guilt-tripping, and the silent treatment. These tactics create confusion, dependency, and self-doubt.

Example: John often tells his partner, Lisa, that she 'remembers things wrong' whenever she points out his hurtful behaviour. Over time, Lisa begins doubting her own memory, feeling insecure and dependent on John's version of events. This is an example of gaslighting, which erodes a person's confidence in their perceptions.

Case Study: Steve has a friend who frequently uses guilt to get him to do favours, saying things like, "I thought I meant more to you than this." Steve ends up feeling obligated to meet his friend's demands, even when it disrupts his life. Manipulation like this creates emotional exhaustion and a one-sided relationship.

9.5 SETTING BOUNDARIES TO PROTECT EMOTIONAL WELL-BEING

Setting boundaries means defining what behaviours are acceptable and protecting oneself from overstepping. Boundaries are crucial in limiting the negative effects of toxic relationships and ensuring personal well-being.

Example: Marie has a colleague who often unloads extra tasks on her. To manage her workload, Marie decides to set a boundary and informs her colleague that she will only take on agreed-upon assignments. Though the colleague initially pushes back, Marie's boundary helps her maintain a balanced work environment.

Case Study: Tom's family members frequently call him late at night to discuss family issues. This disrupts his sleep, affecting his work the next day. Tom sets a boundary by asking his family to call him during daytime hours only. Although they initially resist, Tom's consistency helps them respect his time, allowing him to rest without guilt.

9.6 COPING STRATEGIES FOR MANAGING TOXIC RELATIONSHIPS

When dealing with a toxic relationship, coping strategies are vital for emotional stability. Techniques like practising self-care, setting mental boundaries, or seeking outside support help manage the effects of toxicity.

Example: Alice's partner often criticises her appearance. To cope, Alice focuses on building self-esteem through hobbies she loves, like painting. She also surrounds herself with supportive friends who remind her of her worth. This approach allows Alice to maintain her self-image despite the negativity in her relationship.

Case Study: Leo has a sibling who often brings up his past mistakes to make him feel guilty. Leo starts journaling about his feelings and joins a support group where he learns coping skills. This external support helps Leo process his emotions healthily and reduces the impact of his sibling's behaviour on his mental health.

9.7 ENDING A TOXIC RELATIONSHIP

Leaving a toxic relationship can be challenging, as emotional bonds, fears, or obligations often complicate the process. Planning an exit strategy and leaning on support can help individuals move forward.

Example: Molly is in a relationship where her partner frequently belittles her. After realising how much it affects her, she decides to leave but fears the loneliness that might follow. With the encouragement of friends and a counsellor, Molly prepares herself emotionally and practically, finding her own space and focusing on personal growth after leaving.

Case Study: Jason decides to end his friendship with a longtime friend who consistently uses him for favours and doesn't reciprocate. He reduces contact gradually, focusing on other friendships. This shift allows him to maintain boundaries while reducing guilt, ultimately helping him move on from the relationship with minimal disruption.

9.8 HEALING AND REBUILDING AFTER LEAVING A TOXIC RELATIONSHIP

After ending a toxic relationship, healing is essential to rebuild self-worth, address emotional scars, and restore trust in oneself and others. Therapy, self-reflection, and self-compassion are common tools for recovery.

Example: After leaving a toxic job, James feels a deep sense of self-doubt. He starts therapy, where he works on rebuilding his self-confidence and learning to recognise his strengths. James also reconnects with old hobbies, which help him regain a sense of joy and identity outside his past experiences.

Case Study: Anna ends a friendship with someone who was emotionally abusive. She begins volunteering and taking classes to meet supportive, positive people. This change in environment allows her to focus on new connections and rebuild her social network with healthier boundaries, speeding up her recovery.

9.9 BUILDING HEALTHY RELATIONSHIP PATTERNS FOR THE FUTURE

To prevent future toxicity, individuals can build healthy relationship patterns by setting clear boundaries, communicating openly, and recognising red flags early. Developing self-awareness and assertiveness are key to forming relationships based on mutual respect and trust.

Example: After ending a toxic friendship, Lily commits to setting clear boundaries in future relationships. She practices assertiveness and becomes more mindful of signs of manipulation. As a result, Lily builds friendships based on mutual support, finding it easier to trust and open up to others.

Case Study: Jacob leaves a toxic workplace and actively seeks a healthier environment in his next job, prioritising companies that value open communication and respect. By learning from his past experiences, he ensures his future professional relationships are built on positive values, leading to greater satisfaction and well-being.

These expanded descriptions with examples and case studies should provide a clear, comprehensive understanding of the key topics related to toxic relationships and emotional well-being. Each point demonstrates how individuals can recognise, cope with, and ultimately overcome the effects of toxic relationships, emphasising practical steps and real-life scenarios.

Chapter 10

RESOURCES AND TOOLS

10.1 WORKSHEETS FOR EMOTIONAL DEVELOPMENT

Description: Worksheets can be invaluable tools for children to explore their feelings, understand their emotions, and develop essential skills for emotional intelligence. They provide a structured way for children to articulate their thoughts, reflect on their experiences, and learn to manage their feelings effectively.

Example: One particular worksheet, titled 'Feelings Wheel', allows children to visualise their emotions by selecting from a variety of feelings illustrated around a circle. When young Mia, a 9-year-old, used the worksheet, she initially struggled to identify her emotions. However, as she filled it out, she pointed to 'frustrated' and 'sad' after a difficult day at school. This exercise opened the door for her to discuss her feelings with her mum, leading to a heartwarming conversation about coping strategies.

How to Use:

- Encourage your child to complete the worksheet during calm moments to promote reflection.

- After filling it out, sit down together and discuss the emotions they identified. This fosters an open dialogue and helps normalise conversations about feelings.

Emotional Development Worksheet

Name: _______________________________

Date: _______________________________

Part 1: Feelings Wheel

1.**Draw or colour in the feelings that you experienced today:**

- Happy
- Sad
- Angry
- Frustrated
- Excited
- Scared
- Confused
- Lonely
- Loved
- Hopeful

(Draw a circle around each feeling that you felt today.)

Part 2: Describe Your Feelings

2. **Choose three feelings from your feelings wheel and describe them:**

- **Feeling 1:** _____________________
  - **When did you feel this?** _______________________________
  - **What caused this feeling?** _______________________________
  - **How did you express this feeling?** _______________________

- **Feeling 2:** _________________
    - **When did you feel this?** _________________________
    - **What caused this feeling?** _________________________
    - **How did you express this feeling?** _________________
  - **Feeling 3:** _________________
    - **When did you feel this?** _________________________
    - **What caused this feeling?** _________________________
    - **How did you express this feeling?** _________________

Part 3: Coping Strategies

3. **Think about a time you felt a strong emotion. How did you cope with it?**

    - **What was the emotion?** _________________________
    - **What coping strategies did you use?** _________________
    - **What helped you feel better?** _________________________

Part 4: Daily Affirmation

4. **Write a positive affirmation for yourself:**

    (Example: "I am brave, and I can face my challenges.")

Part 5: Reflection

5. **How can you express your feelings better in the future?**

Instructions for Parents or Caregivers:

- Encourage your child to complete this worksheet during a quiet time.
- Discuss their answers together to foster open communication about feelings.
- Use this worksheet regularly to help your child track their emotional growth.

Emotional Awareness Worksheet

Name: _______________________________________

Date: _______________________________________

Part 1: My Emotion Diary

1. **Reflect on your day. Write down three different emotions you felt today.**

   - **Emotion 1: _______________**
     - **What happened that made you feel this way?**
   - **Emotion 2: _______________**
     - **What happened that made you feel this way?**
   - **Emotion 3: _______________**
     - **What happened that made you feel this way?**

Part 2: Understanding Triggers

2. **Choose one emotion from your diary that you want to understand better.**

   - **Emotion Chosen: _______________**
   - **What usually triggers this emotion for you?**
   - **How do you usually react when you feel this way?**

Part 3: Empathy Practice

3. **Think of a friend or family member. Write down an emotion you think they might be feeling.**

   - **Person's Name: _______________**
   - **Emotion You Think They Are Feeling: _______________**
   - **What might have caused them to feel this way?**

4. **How can you show empathy to this person?**

Part 4: Coping Strategies

1. **Write down at least two strategies you can use to cope with difficult emotions.**

   - **Strategy 1:** _______________________________________
   - **Strategy 2:** _______________________________________

Part 5: Positive Reminder

1. **Create a positive reminder or quote for yourself that you can refer to when you're feeling overwhelmed.**

   (Example: "It's okay to feel this way; I can get through it.")

Instructions for Parents or Caregivers:

- Encourage your child to fill out this worksheet in a calm environment.

- Discuss their reflections and insights together, reinforcing the importance of emotional awareness and empathy.

- Make this worksheet a regular practice to help your child build emotional resilience.

10.2 CHECKLISTS FOR PARENTS AND CAREGIVERS

Description: Checklists serve as practical tools for parents and caregivers to nurture emotional growth in children. They provide actionable steps to ensure that children receive consistent support and guidance.

Example: Consider the 'Daily Emotional Check In Checklist'. Each day, it prompts parents to ask their children about their feelings, encourage self-reflection, and identify coping strategies for any challenges they may face. When Mark, a dedicated dad, implemented this checklist with his 11-year-old daughter, Lily, he discovered that asking simple questions like, "What made you smile today?" or "Did anything upset you?" transformed their nightly routine into a cherished bonding time.

How to Use:

- Place the checklist in a visible location, like on the fridge, as a daily reminder.
- Use it as a starting point for conversations during family dinners or bedtime, creating a safe space for children to express themselves.

Emotional Development Checklist for Parents and Caregivers

Name of Child: _______________________________________

Date: ___________________________________

Daily Emotional Support Checklist

Use this checklist daily to ensure you're providing the emotional support your child needs. Check the box for each task you complete.

Task	Check
1. **Ask your child about their feelings today.** *"How was your day? What made you happy today?"*	☐
2. **Encourage your child to express themselves.** *Allow them to talk about their emotions without judgement.*	☐
3. **Spend quality time together.** *Engage in an activity your child enjoys, like reading, playing games, or cooking.*	☐

Task	Check
4. **Use feeling words.** *Model emotional vocabulary by describing your own feelings..*	☐
5. **Teach coping strategies.** *Discuss breathing exercises, mindfulness, or calming techniques.*	☐
6. **Encourage problem-solving.** *Help your child think through challenges they face and brainstorm solutions.*	☐
7. **Share positive affirmations.** *Remind your child of their strengths and the things they do well.*	☐
8. **Practice empathy together.** *Discuss how others might feel in different situations and how to respond kindly.*	☐
9. **Check in on their friendships.** *Ask about their friends and any social interactions they had during the day.*	☐
10. **Reflect on the day.** *At bedtime, have a short chat about what went well and what could be improved tomorrow.*	☐

Weekly Reflection

At the end of the week, reflect on your child's emotional development:

1. **What emotions did your child express most frequently this week?**

____

2. **What strategies were most effective in supporting your child›s emotional needs?**

____

3. **Did you notice any changes in your child›s emotional responses? If so, what were they?**

____

Instructions for Parents and Caregivers:

- Use this checklist daily to stay aware of your child's emotional needs.

- At the end of each week, review your reflections to adapt your approach, as necessary.

- Make this a family routine to foster open communication and emotional growth.

10.3 ACTIVITIES FOR DAILY PRACTICE

Description: Engaging in daily emotional intelligence activities can be a fun and effective way to reinforce skills learned. These activities promote awareness, empathy, and emotional regulation in a playful manner.

Example: One such activity is 'Emotion Charades', where family members take turns acting out different emotions while others guess. When the Rodriguez family played this game, their 7-year-old son, Alex, initially hesitated to participate. However, as he watched his parents dramatically act out feelings like 'frustration' and 'joy', he began to join in. Laughter filled the room as he mimicked 'excitement' with exaggerated jumps, and in that joyful moment, Alex not only learned to recognise emotions but also developed confidence in expressing his own.

How to Use:

- Incorporate this activity into family game nights to make it enjoyable.

- After each round, discuss why certain actions represented specific emotions, deepening the understanding of feelings.

10.4 DAILY EMOTIONAL INTELLIGENCE ACTIVITIES

Activity 1: Emotion Diary

Objective: To encourage children to reflect on their daily emotions.

Instructions:

- Each evening, ask your child to write down three emotions they felt that day and what caused them.

- Encourage them to draw or use stickers to represent their feelings.

Analysis Sheet:

Day	Emotion	What Caused It?	How Did I Cope?	What Can I Do Next Time?
Monday				
Tuesday				
Wednesday				
Thursday				
Friday				

Activity 2: Feelings Charades

Objective: To help children recognise and express emotions through body language.

Instructions:

- Write down different emotions on slips of paper (e.g., happy, sad, angry, surprised).
- Take turns drawing a slip and acting out the emotion without speaking while others guess.

Analysis Sheet:

Emotion	How Did I Act It Out?	How Did Others Respond?	What Did I Learn About This Emotion?

Activity 3: Kindness Challenge

Objective: To foster empathy and kindness in daily interactions.

Instructions:

- Challenge your child to perform one act of kindness each day (e.g., helping a friend, complimenting someone, sharing).

Analysis Sheet:

Day	Act of Kindness	How Did It Make Me Feel?	How Did the Other Person React?	What Did I Learn?
Monday				
Tuesday				
Wednesday				
Thursday				
Friday				

Activity 4: Mindfulness Moments

Objective: To teach children mindfulness and emotional regulation.

Instructions:

- Set aside 5-10 minutes daily for mindfulness exercises such as deep breathing, guided imagery, or simple meditation.

- After the exercise, ask your child how they felt before and after.

Analysis Sheet:

Day	Mindfulness Exercise	How Did I Feel Before?	How Did I Feel After?	What Techniques Helped?
Monday				
Tuesday				
Wednesday				
Thursday				
Friday				

Instructions for Parents and Caregivers:

- Encourage your child to engage in one or more of these activities daily.

- Use the accompanying analysis sheets at the end of the week to review their experiences and reflect on their emotional growth.

- Discuss what they learned from each activity to reinforce their understanding of emotions and coping strategies.

10.4 THE IMPORTANCE OF WORKSHEETS AND ANALYSIS SHEETS IN FOSTERING EMOTIONAL INTELLIGENCE

1. Emotion Diary

Importance:

- **Self-Reflection**: The Emotion Diary encourages children to reflect on their daily experiences, fostering self-awareness. By recognising their emotions, children learn to identify what affects their mood and behaviour.

- **Emotional Vocabulary**: Regularly writing down feelings helps children expand their emotional vocabulary, making it easier for them to articulate their emotions in the future.

- **Coping Strategies**: The analysis section prompts children to think about how they cope with various feelings, helping them develop healthier responses and coping mechanisms.

2. Feelings Charades

Importance:

- **Non-Verbal Communication**: This activity highlights the importance of body language and non-verbal cues in expressing emotions. It teaches children to recognise how emotions can be conveyed without words.

- **Empathy Development**: As children act out emotions and guess others' feelings, they build empathy and understanding, realising that everyone experiences a range of emotions.

- **Social Skills**: Engaging in group activities enhances social interactions and teamwork, vital for developing strong relationships.

3. Kindness Challenge

Importance:

- **Promoting Empathy**: The Kindness Challenge encourages children to step outside themselves and consider the feelings of others. Performing acts of kindness fosters empathy and strengthens social bonds.

- **Positive Reinforcement**: Reflecting on how kindness makes both the giver and receiver feel reinforces positive behaviour and encourages a habit of kindness.

- **Building Resilience**: Engaging in acts of kindness can improve a child's self-esteem and emotional resilience, making them feel empowered and valued.

4. Mindfulness Moments

Importance:

- **Emotional Regulation**: Mindfulness exercises help children learn to manage their emotions by teaching them to pause and reflect before reacting. This skill is crucial for emotional regulation.

- **Stress Reduction**: Practising mindfulness can reduce anxiety and stress, promoting a sense of calm and well-being.

- **Focus and Attention**: Mindfulness activities enhance concentration and attention, allowing children to better engage with their surroundings and cope with emotional challenges.

Analysis Sheets

General Importance

- **Track Progress**: The analysis sheets associated with each activity allow parents and children to track emotional growth over time. Recognising patterns in emotions can lead to better understanding and management of feelings.

- **Reflective Learning**: Reflection encourages deeper learning. By analysing their feelings, responses, and interactions, children learn valuable lessons about emotional intelligence.

- **Facilitate Communication**: The structured format of the analysis sheets provides a foundation for conversations between parents and children about feelings, fostering open dialogue and strengthening relationships.

Specific Importance of Each Analysis Sheet

1. **Emotion Diary Analysis Sheet**:
   - Helps identify recurring emotions and their triggers, guiding parents in providing appropriate support.

2. **Feelings Charades Analysis Sheet**:
   - Encourages children to consider how their emotions affect interactions with others, enhancing emotional literacy.

3. **Kindness Challenge Analysis Sheet**:
   - Promotes reflection on the impact of kindness, reinforcing the positive effects of altruistic behaviour on both self and others.

4. **Mindfulness Moments Analysis Sheet**:

   - Assesses the effectiveness of mindfulness techniques, allowing adjustments to be made for better emotional regulation.

Conclusion

Overall, these worksheets and analysis sheets are powerful tools for fostering emotional intelligence in children. They promote self-awareness, empathy, emotional regulation, and positive social interactions. By engaging in these activities and using the accompanying analysis sheets, children learn to navigate their emotional landscapes effectively, setting a solid foundation for lifelong emotional health and resilience. Additionally, parents and caregivers can gain insights into their child's emotional needs, facilitating stronger connections and support systems.

Chapter 11

BUILDING RESILIENCE

11.1 UNDERSTANDING RESILIENCE

Resilience refers to the capacity to recover from difficulties and adapt to challenging situations. It is not merely about enduring hardships but also about developing the ability to thrive in the face of adversity. Understanding resilience involves recognising it as a dynamic process that encompasses various skills and behaviours, which can be cultivated over time. Children who develop resilience are better equipped to handle stress, navigate obstacles, and emerge from challenging experiences with newfound strength. Parents play a crucial role in this process by providing a supportive environment that encourages open communication, problem-solving, and emotional expression.

11.2 STRATEGIES FOR DEVELOPING A GROWTH MINDSET

A growth mindset is the belief that abilities can be developed through dedication and hard work. To foster this mindset in children, parents and caregivers can employ several strategies. Encouraging a love for learning is essential; by praising effort rather than innate talent, children learn that persistence and resilience are valuable traits. They should also be taught to embrace challenges and view obstacles as opportunities for growth rather than threats to their abilities. By instilling a belief that effort leads to improvement, parents can empower children to approach life with a sense of curiosity and a willingness to learn from their experiences.

11.3 LEARNING FROM FAILURES AND SETBACKS

Experiencing failure is a natural part of life that can serve as a powerful teacher. Teaching children to view setbacks not as the end but as an opportunity for growth is essential for building resilience. Parents can encourage children to reflect on their experiences by asking guiding questions: What went wrong? What can I learn from this? How can I approach the situation differently next time? By framing failure as a valuable learning experience, children can develop a mindset that embraces challenges and persists in the face of adversity, ultimately fostering a more resilient attitude toward life.

11.4 MAINTAINING A POSITIVE OUTLOOK

Maintaining a positive outlook is crucial for emotional resilience, as it enables children to cope with stress and adversity more effectively. Parents can support their children in cultivating this outlook by modelling positive thinking in their own lives and encouraging gratitude practices. For instance, keeping a gratitude journal can help children focus on the positive aspects of their lives, even in challenging times. Engaging in discussions about uplifting experiences and future possibilities can further reinforce a sense of hope and optimism. By fostering a positive mindset, parents help children build a protective buffer against the stresses of life.

Chapter 12

FOSTERING HEALTHY RELATIONSHIPS

12.1 BUILDING AND MAINTAINING POSITIVE CONNECTIONS

Healthy relationships are foundational to emotional well-being and resilience. Encouraging children to develop friendships based on mutual respect and support is vital for their social development. Parents can facilitate this by providing opportunities for children to engage with peers through group activities, such as team sports, clubs, or community events. Open communication is also essential; children should feel comfortable discussing their feelings and experiences with friends and family. By nurturing these positive connections, children learn valuable social skills that contribute to their emotional health and resilience.

12.2 SETTING AND RESPECTING BOUNDARIES

Teaching children about boundaries is essential for developing healthy relationships. Parents should explain the importance of personal space and consent, helping children understand that their feelings and needs are valid. Encouraging children to express their boundaries clearly fosters assertiveness and respect for others' boundaries. By modelling healthy boundary-setting in their own relationships, parents provide a concrete example for children to follow. This understanding of boundaries not only protects children from potential harm but also enhances their ability to engage in respectful, healthy interactions with others.

12.3 NAVIGATING SOCIAL DYNAMICS

Social interactions can often be complex and challenging for children. Teaching them to recognise social cues, body language, and emotional expressions is essential for successful interactions. Parents can help children develop conflict resolution skills, guiding them to handle disagreements respectfully and constructively. Role-playing various social scenarios can provide children with the practice they need to navigate social dynamics confidently. By equipping children with these skills, parents empower them to build positive relationships and effectively manage social challenges, ultimately enhancing their emotional intelligence.

Chapter 13

PROMOTING MENTAL
AND PHYSICAL HEALTH

13.1 THE IMPORTANCE OF PHYSICAL ACTIVITY

Regular physical activity is crucial for maintaining both mental and physical health. Engaging in exercise helps children reduce stress, improve mood, and boost overall well-being. Parents can encourage children to be active by promoting various forms of physical activity, such as sports, dancing, or outdoor play. It's essential to help children find activities they enjoy, as this increases the likelihood of maintaining a consistent routine. Family activities, such as hiking, biking, or playing games together, can also strengthen family bonds while promoting a healthy lifestyle. By prioritising physical activity, parents lay the groundwork for their children's long-term health and resilience.

13.2 ENCOURAGING HEALTHY EATING HABITS

Nutrition plays a vital role in emotional and physical health, making it essential for parents to promote healthy eating habits in children. Educating children about the benefits of a balanced diet, which includes fruits, vegetables, whole grains, and proteins, can help them make informed food choices. Involving children in meal planning and preparation not only fosters a greater appreciation for healthy foods but also teaches them valuable life skills. When parents model healthy eating habits and make nutritious food choices themselves, they create a positive environment that encourages children to adopt similar habits. This foundational knowledge and practice contribute to better overall health and emotional well-being.

13.3 ENSURING SUFFICIENT SLEEP

Adequate sleep is crucial for children's emotional regulation, cognitive function, and overall health. Parents can help their children develop healthy sleep habits by establishing a consistent bedtime routine that promotes relaxation and winding down before sleep. Limiting screen time before bed and creating a comfortable sleep environment free from distractions are also important steps. Teaching children about the importance of sleep and its impact on their mood and energy levels can help them understand the need for adequate rest. By prioritising sufficient sleep, parents support their children's emotional resilience and overall well-being.

13.4 ACCESSING MENTAL HEALTH RESOURCES

Being proactive about mental health is essential for children's emotional development. Parents should educate themselves about the signs of emotional distress and be prepared to seek professional help when necessary. Providing children with access to mental health resources, such as counselling, support groups, or therapy, can help them navigate challenges effectively. Encouraging open conversations about mental health reduces stigma and normalises seeking help. By fostering an environment where mental health is prioritised and discussed, parents can empower their children to take charge of their emotional well-being and seek support when needed.

Chapter 14

CONCLUSION

14.1 THE LONG-TERM BENEFITS OF EMOTIONAL INTELLIGENCE AND RESILIENCE

Investing in emotional intelligence and resilience provides children with lifelong skills that positively impact their lives. Developing emotional intelligence enables children to understand and manage their emotions effectively, enhancing their ability to build and maintain relationships. Resilience equips them to handle stress and adversity, allowing them to bounce back from challenges and setbacks with a growth mindset. The skills acquired through nurturing emotional intelligence and resilience contribute to success in academic and professional endeavours and overall mental health, making them invaluable assets for a fulfilling life.

The long-term benefits of fostering emotional intelligence (EI) and resilience in children are profound, shaping not only their immediate personal development but also laying the groundwork for successful and fulfilling lives as adults. Emotional intelligence equips individuals with the ability to recognise, understand, and manage their own emotions, as well as empathise with the emotions of others. These skills are essential for building strong, meaningful relationships, which can positively influence nearly every aspect of life, from family connections to friendships and professional success.

One of the major long-term benefits of emotional intelligence is improved mental health. Emotionally intelligent individuals are better equipped to handle stress, anxiety, and emotional setbacks. They are less likely to suppress emotions, which can lead to psychological issues if left unaddressed, and more likely to employ healthy coping mechanisms such as problem-solving, mindfulness, and positive reframing. These practices not only reduce the risk of developing mental health issues but also foster resilience—the ability to recover from difficulties and adapt to changing circumstances. Resilient individuals are less likely to feel overwhelmed by life's challenges, which can improve both their mental and physical well-being over time.

In personal relationships, emotional intelligence and resilience contribute to effective communication, empathy, and conflict resolution skills. People with high emotional intelligence can navigate social dynamics with ease, recognising and validating others' feelings while expressing their own needs constructively. This empathy-driven approach helps build deeper, more trusting relationships and reduces misunderstandings. In romantic relationships and close friendships, these skills are particularly valuable for fostering intimacy and mutual respect, creating a supportive network that acts as a buffer against life's inevitable stresses.

In the workplace, emotional intelligence is often a predictor of career success. It enhances teamwork, leadership, and adaptability—all crucial skills in today's rapidly evolving professional environments. Emotionally intelligent employees are more likely to navigate workplace challenges effectively, whether it's managing stress, handling feedback constructively, or motivating themselves and others. Those with high

EI are also typically strong leaders, as they can inspire and connect with team members on a personal level, motivating them to achieve common goals. This capability makes EI a highly sought-after quality in leadership positions, as it contributes to a positive, collaborative work culture and helps retain talent by ensuring that employees feel valued and understood.

Resilience complements emotional intelligence by enabling individuals to maintain a positive outlook and adapt to adversity. Resilient individuals are less likely to dwell on setbacks, instead focusing on solutions and growth opportunities. This adaptability not only supports them through personal challenges but also increases their capacity to seize opportunities for personal and professional development. The combination of EI and resilience encourages lifelong learning and the ability to persevere, both of which are essential for adapting to life's changes and pursuing long-term goals.

Ultimately, emotional intelligence and resilience together build a foundation for overall life satisfaction. These skills promote a balanced approach to life, where emotional well-being, social connections, and personal growth are valued alongside achievements. By prioritising emotional health and resilience from an early age, individuals are better prepared to navigate the ups and downs of life with confidence, empathy, and optimism, which contributes to a fulfilling, resilient, and emotionally healthy life trajectory.

14.2 FINAL THOUGHTS AND ENCOURAGEMENT FOR PARENTS AND CAREGIVERS

Parents play a pivotal role in nurturing emotional intelligence and resilience in their children. By modelling these traits, fostering supportive environments, and encouraging open dialogue about feelings, parents can empower their children to thrive emotionally and socially. It is essential to remain patient and understanding as children navigate their emotional development, celebrating their progress while providing guidance and support. Encouraging ongoing conversations about challenges and successes strengthens the parent-child bond and reinforces the importance of emotional well-being. As parents and caregivers, the journey of nurturing a child's emotional growth and resilience is both deeply rewarding and filled with unique challenges. The guidance you provide today will leave a lasting imprint on your child's ability to navigate life's complexities, form healthy relationships, and face setbacks with courage. It's natural to feel uncertain or even overwhelmed at times, as there is no single formula for parenting, and each child has their own personality, strengths, and needs. However, the consistent love, understanding, and guidance you offer can be one of the most powerful tools in helping your child grow into a confident, emotionally healthy individual.

One of the most valuable aspects of this journey is remembering that no parent or caregiver is perfect—and that's okay. Children learn just as much from witnessing their caregivers' vulnerabilities and challenges as they do from their successes. When you model self-compassion and a willingness to learn, you demonstrate that it's okay to make mistakes, adapt, and grow. This teaches children a vital lesson about resilience and self-acceptance, encouraging them to approach their own mistakes with kindness rather than criticism. In times of frustration or stress, taking a moment to reflect on what you hope to instil in your child can help ground you in your long-term goals for their emotional and personal development.

A key part of supporting your child is creating a safe and open environment where they feel free to express their feelings without fear of judgement. By listening actively, validating their emotions, and offering reassurance, you cultivate a relationship where they know they are supported. This emotional security is foundational to their sense of self-worth and confidence, allowing them to face the world with a strong, positive self-image. Additionally, through ongoing, open communication, you become a trusted resource in their lives, someone they can turn to for guidance as they grow and encounter new situations.

It's also important to remember that small, consistent actions have a cumulative effect. Encouraging self-expression, teaching empathy, modelling emotional regulation, and fostering resilience do not need to happen all at once. Daily interactions, whether it's discussing their day at the dinner table or comforting them after a disappointment, build an emotional foundation over time. The patience and care you invest in these moments lay the groundwork for them to develop emotional intelligence, self-confidence, and a healthy approach to challenges.

Equipping your child with skills to handle peer pressure, process disappointment, and embrace individuality empowers them to make choices aligned with their values and strengths. While you can't shield them from every difficulty, you can give them tools to face these moments with resilience. Sharing stories from your own life, teaching problem-solving skills, and encouraging self-reflection can all help them feel capable of overcoming obstacles. Embracing a growth mindset also reminds them that setbacks are a natural part of life and an opportunity to learn and grow.

In the end, trust that the love, encouragement, and guidance you offer will carry forward into your child's future, even in ways you may not immediately see. Every lesson in empathy, every opportunity to listen and validate their emotions, and every moment of shared connection strengthens their emotional resilience. Take pride in the role you play in shaping their lives, knowing that your dedication contributes to their happiness and ability to thrive. Parenting is a journey that grows with each step, and your presence and commitment have an immeasurable impact. The support you provide now will echo throughout your child's life, enabling them to face the world with confidence, compassion, and resilience.

Chapter 15

APPENDICES

Appendix A: Emotional Intelligence Self-Assessment for Parents

This self-assessment tool helps parents evaluate their emotional intelligence skills, providing insight into areas for personal growth. The assessment includes questions related to self-awareness, self-regulation, empathy, and social skills.

Appendix B: Resilience-Building Activities

A list of simple activities and exercises designed for parents and children to practise together, such as:

- **Gratitude Journaling**: Encouraging children to write down three things they are grateful for each day.

- **Story Sharing**: Sharing personal stories of overcoming challenges to inspire resilience.

- **Mindfulness Exercises**: Guided practices for relaxation and emotional regulation.

Appendix C: Family Communication Guidelines

Guidelines for establishing open communication within the family. This could include:

- Creating a 'feelings corner' at home where family members can express their emotions freely.

- Setting aside regular family meetings to discuss feelings and resolve conflicts.

- Tips for active listening and validating each other's feelings.

15.1 ADDITIONAL RESOURCES

Books

1. **'The Whole-Brain Child' by Daniel J. Siegel and Tina Payne Bryson**: A practical guide for parents on how to nurture their child's developing mind and promote emotional intelligence.

2. **'Mindset: The New Psychology of Success' by Carol S. Dweck**: Explores the concept of a growth mindset and its impact on children's resilience and achievement.

3. **'Raising Resilient Children' by Robert Brooks and Sam Goldstein**: Offers strategies and insights for parents to help their children build resilience.

Websites

1. **The Greater Good Science Centre (greatergood.berkeley.edu)**: Provides research-based resources on social and emotional well-being, including articles and tools for parents and educators.

2. **The Child Mind Institute (childmind.org)**: A nonprofit organisation dedicated to transforming the lives of children and families struggling with mental health and learning disorders. It offers resources, articles, and support for parents.

3. **Zero to Three (zerotothree.org)**: A national nonprofit organisation that provides parents with information on child

development and parenting resources to foster emotional and social skills.

Online Courses and Workshops

1. **Emotional Intelligence Courses on Coursera**: Offers a variety of courses on emotional intelligence that can benefit both parents and educators.

2. **Mindfulness for Parents by Mindful Schools**: Online classes focused on incorporating mindfulness into parenting, helping parents model emotional regulation for their children.

Helplines and Support Services

1. **National Parent Helpline (1-855-427-2736)**: Provides emotional support and advocacy for parents in need.

2. **Substance Abuse and Mental Health Services Administration (SAMHSA) National Helpline (1-800-662-HELP)**: A confidential, free, 24/7 treatment referral and information service for individuals and families facing mental health and substance use disorders.

Chapter 16

REFERENCES

- **Books**
  - Siegel, D. J., & Bryson, T. P. (2011). *The Whole-Brain Child: 12 Revolutionary Strategies to Nurture Your Child's Developing Mind.* Bantam Books.
  - Dweck, C. S. (2006). *Mindset: The New Psychology of Success.* Random House.
  - Brooks, R., & Goldstein, S. (2004). *Raising Resilient Children: Fostering Strength, Hope, and Optimism in Your Child.* McGraw-Hill.
- **Websites**
  - Greater Good Science Centre. (n.d.). Retrieved from https://greatergood.berkeley.edu
  - Child Mind Institute. (n.d.). Retrieved from https://childmind.org
  - Zero to Three. (n.d.). Retrieved from https://zerotothree.org
- **Online Courses and Workshops.**

- Coursera. (n.d.). Emotional Intelligence Courses. Retrieved from https://www.coursera.org/courses?query=emotional%20 intelligence

- Mindful Schools. (n.d.). Mindfulness for Parents. Retrieved from https://www.mindfulschools.org

- **Helplines and Support Services**

- National Parent Helpline. (n.d.). Retrieved from https://www. nationalparenthelpline.org

- Substance Abuse and Mental Health Services Administration (SAMHSA) National Helpline. (n.d.). Retrieved from https:// www.samhsa.gov/find-help/national-helpline

Chapter 17

INDEX

A

D

E

F

G

H

L

M

N

O

P

R

S

- Setting and Respecting Boundaries
- Self-Esteem
- Siegel, Daniel J.

T

- The Importance of Physical Activity
- The Whole-Brain Child

U

- Understanding Resilience

W

- Worksheets for Emotional Development
- Websites for Further Resources